Magic
for Everybody

250 Easy Tricks
with Cards, Coins, Rings,
Handkerchiefs and Other Objects

JOSEPH LEEMING

Dover Publications, Inc.
Mineola, New York

Bibliographical Note

This Dover edition, first published in 2007, is an unabridged republication of the work originally published in 1928 by Doubleday, Doran & Co., Garden City, N.Y., under the title *Magic for Everybody: The 250 Best and Newest Feats of Magic Chosen for the Ease with Which They Can Be Performed.*

International Standard Book Number
ISBN-13: 978-0-486-46146-5
ISBN-10: 0-486-46146-7

Manufactured in the United States of America
Dover Publications, Inc., 31 East 2nd Street, Mineola, N.Y. 11501

DEDICATED TO
BILL AND PETER DOUGLAS

FOREWORD

Every trick in this book has been chosen for two qualities—the maximum of effectiveness and mystification and the minimum requirement of skill or sleight of hand. Simplicity in execution has been kept in mind throughout, so that any and every one will be able to perform all the tricks in the book after a short period of practice. No elaborate apparatus is needed in connection with any of the tricks, and most of them can be performed at any time and at any place with the common objects which can always be obtained.

CONTENTS

TRICKS WITH RINGS

TRICKS WITH CARDS

TRICKS WITH MATCHES

TRICKS WITH HANDKERCHIEFS

TRICKS WITH CIGARS AND CIGARETTES

TRICKS WITH NUMBERS

Tricks with Dice and Dominoes

Experiments in Magnetism

CONTENTS

CONTENTS

TRICKS WITH GLASSES

MISCELLANEOUS TRICKS

TRICKS WITH RINGS

THE DISAPPEARING RING

THIS is one of the simplest methods to cause a
ring or coin to disappear when you are performing without apparatus or in a strange house.

Get a small rubber band, or if one of the small size
is not obtainable, use an ordinary sized one and
double it to make it smaller. The rubber band is
secretly placed over the thumb and forefinger of the
left hand, and a handkerchief is thrown over the
hand to cover it. The ring is then placed in the center
of the handkerchief, the thumb and forefinger of the
left hand grasp it through the handkerchief and slip
the rubber band over it, thus enclosing it in a little
pocket whose mouth is closed by the rubber band. A
pretense may be made of folding the handkerchief

over the ring while the rubber band is being adjusted. The right hand then grasps one corner of the handkerchief, shakes it out, and the ring has vanished.

THE FLYING RING

THIS is an instantaneous and invisible flight of a ring, which has been featured by many noted magicians. In effect, the performer takes a ring in his left hand and throws it into the air, where it vanishes, only to reappear instantly on one of the fingers of the right hand.

Two rings are used, which are duplicates. If a ring is borrowed from the audience, which makes the trick more effective, it should be a wedding ring, and the performer should provide himself with an imitation wedding ring from the ten-cent store. This ring is attached to one end of a piece of string, which is led up the left sleeve, across the back, and down the right sleeve to the wrist, where it is secured.

The borrowed ring is taken in the right hand and is apparently transferred to the left. It is, however, really retained in the right hand, and the duplicate ring is exhibited at the left fingertips. The borrowed ring is hung on a small hook of the hook-and-eye variety, which is sewed to the right side of the performer's trousers just above the pocket. The right hand can now be shown empty, yet, as soon as the duplicate ring has been vanished by extending the left arm and permitting it to be drawn up the sleeve, the performer can take the original ring from its convenient hiding place and slip it on one of the fingers on his right hand.

THE KNOTTED RING ON STRING TRICK

IN THIS trick the performer's wrists are tied together, the ends of a piece of string being knotted around his wrists, and a length of about two feet being left between the wrists. When this has been done, he borrows a ring and turns his back for a moment. When he turns around the ring is securely knotted to the middle of the string.

The trick is accomplished as follows: Push the center of the length of string hanging between the wrists through the ring, thus forming a loop. Slip this loop over the right hand and wrist, bringing it to a point below the string which already encircles the wrist. Then pull it underneath the string encircling the wrist and bring it back over the hand, passing it from the back of the hand to the front. The ring will then be knotted in such a way that the string will have to be cut or untied to remove it.

PASSING A RING THROUGH A
HANDKERCHIEF

A BORROWED ring is wrapped up in a handkerchief, the ends of the handkerchief being tied together so that the ring cannot possibly fall out. This handkerchief is given to a member of the audience to hold, and the performer places another handkerchief over it. Reaching under the second handkerchief for a moment, he withdraws his hand, in which reposes the borrowed ring. In some mysterious manner it has been drawn right through the folds of the handkerchief.

Before showing the trick the magician conceals a ring of his own in his left hand. This ring is simply a piece of quite stiff wire bent into circular shape and with both of its ends filed to a point. The borrowed ring is taken in the right hand and placed in the left together with the prepared ring. The handkerchief is then thrown over the performer's right hand, and the prepared ring is dropped into it, the audience, of course, believing it to be the original ring. Under cover of the second handkerchief, one of the pointed ends of the prepared ring is forced through the handkerchief, and the ring is extricated. It is taken in the right hand and concealed there when the hands are withdrawn, the original ring being brought out in the open palm of the left hand.

THE TRAVELING RING

THE performer's wrists are securely bound to-gether behind his back. He then seats himself on a chair, and the audience ties him to it as tightly as possible. Now a ring is placed in his teeth and a screen is placed in front of him. The audience tell him on which finger of which hand they wish the ring to appear, and when the screen is removed it is found on the correct finger, though the performer is still tied as tightly as before.

The only possible explanation would seem to be that the performer in some way frees one of his hands so that he can bring it to his mouth, but the trick is not done in this way. It is far simpler. The ring is merely dropped into the performer's lap and from there onto the seat of the chair. Lifting his body slightly, he edges it back until his hands can reach it, and it is then put on whichever finger the audience select.

THE ENCHANTED RING

THE enchanted ring is one of the most puzzling tricks that any performer can show his audience. A string is passed through the center of a ring, and one or two spectators are given the ends to hold. A handkerchief is placed over the ring, the performer reaches under it for an instant, and then removes the handkerchief, when the ring is seen to be tied to the string. The handkerchief is replaced, and the performer reaches under it again and immediately withdraws his hand, holding in it the ring, which has mysteriously been pulled right off the string in spite of the tight grip on the ends maintained by the spectators.

The secret of the trick lies in the use of two similar rings, one of which the performer has concealed in his right hand before commencing the trick. When he reaches under the handkerchief the first time, he "ties" the concealed ring to the string by passing a loop of string through its center and drawing it back over the ring's sides. He then covers the original ring with one of his hands and removes the handkerchief with the other hand, when the audience see the duplicate ring tied to the string, though they naturally believe it to be the original one. Now the performer places the hand that removed the handkerchief on the string and slides both hands to the ends, taking them away from the spectators for an instant and holding the string up so that everybody can see it. Before returning it to the spectators, he slips the original ring off the string entirely and conceals it in his hand. The handkerchief is replaced, and with his free hand the performer reaches under, disengages the loop, and produces the mysteriously freed ring.

THE RING AND PENCIL TRICK

A BORROWED ring is wrapped in a handkerchief and given to one of the audience to hold. The performer then borrows a pencil and gives it to another spectator, who holds it by the ends. A handkerchief is thrown over the pencil. The performer then grasps a corner of each handkerchief, the one enfolding the ring and the one covering the pencil, and gives each a sharp pull. The ring has vanished from the handkerchief and has mysteriously gotten onto the pencil.

The magician must prepare for this trick by sewing a plain ring in one corner of a handkerchief and covering it with a piece of the same material so that it will not be visible. When he wraps up the borrowed ring, he really retains it in his hand and wraps up the sewed-in ring instead. He then borrows a pencil and, while walking back to his table, slips the borrowed ring onto its center, holding the ring between his thumb and first two fingers, the thumb being uppermost. In this position the ring will be completely hidden from sight, and the performer's grip on the pencil will look perfectly natural. As soon as the handkerchief is thrown over the pencil the magician removes his hand, but not before, and the trick is brought to a rapid conclusion lest the person holding the pencil tilt it and discover the hidden ring.

THE DISSOLVING RINGS

THIS is one of the newest and most baffling ring tricks and one that it will pay the amateur to practise until he is letter perfect, as it will never fail thoroughly to mystify an audience when it is capably presented.

Several rings are borrowed from the audience, and the largest is securely tied in the middle of a long piece of string. The other rings are then threaded over the two ends of the string by the audience, so that they rest on top of the first ring. Two spectators hold the ends of the string, and a handkerchief is thrown over the rings. The performer holds one hand palm upward beneath the rings and reaches under the handkerchief for an instant with the other hand. Almost instantly the rings fall out into his outstretched palm, having been mysteriously released from the string.

The way in which the first ring is secured to the center of the string is the crux of this trick. The string is doubled and the looped end is pushed through the ring. The two ends are then passed through the loop and pulled as far as possible, thus securing the ring in a loop. Though this appears to be a perfectly tight knot, it can be undone in a moment by simply drawing the loop down over the ring. The string will then pass through the center of the ring, and all the rings will be disengaged and fall into the performer's hand.

TRICKS WITH CARDS

AN EASY WAY TO MAKE THE PASS

IN MANY card tricks it is necessary to have the audience choose a card, return it to the deck, and then get it on top of the deck, from which it can be readily removed or gotten hold of when required. The easiest and least detectable method of getting a chosen card to the top of the deck is described herewith.

When the spectator is about to return his card, the performer cuts the deck, retaining the lower portion in his left hand and removing the upper portion with his right hand. The spectator then places his card on top of the lower portion, and the performer immediately replaces the upper portion, but crooks the little finger of his left hand between the two halves of the deck. In this position the deck can be held naturally in the left hand, and it will look as though the two halves of the deck had been really reunited.

The next move is the natural one of shuffling the cards "to make sure that the chosen card is thoroughly lost in the deck." But in shuffling, the performer takes all the upper portion of the deck, which is separated from the lower portion by his little finger, in his right hand, and shuffles it back onto the lower portion of the deck, in this way leaving the chosen card on top. There are no rapid movements made during the whole execution of the sleight and the more naturally and easily the processes are carried out, the less the audience will suspect. The performer can then continue shuffling by using the false shuffle described below.

THE FALSE SHUFFLE

TO SHUFFLE the deck after a chosen card has been brought to the top by means of the pass, and to keep the chosen card in this position during the shuffling, is easily accomplished by means of the false shuffle described herewith.

In executing this sleight, the performer holds the deck in his left hand in the same position as for an ordinary shuffle and with the faces of the cards facing toward the left. When ready to shuffle, he removes the bulk of the center of the pack with his right hand, retaining a few of the top and bottom cards between the fingers and thumb of his left hand. The center cards are then promptly shuffled back onto the front of the deck in the ordinary way, and the motion is executed several times in succession. This is a simple sleight which can easily be mastered with a few minutes' practice, but it adds immeàsurably to the effect of all card tricks in which it is necessary to make the pass, bring a chosen card to the top of the deck, and keep it there for future use.

LOCATING A CHOSEN CARD

AN EXCELLENT way to find a chosen card, and one which involves no sleight of hand whatever, is as follows. After the pack has been shuffled, the performer secretly notes and remembers the bottom card. He then puts the cards face down on the table in six piles, being careful to remember which pile contains the bottom card. One of the spectators is then asked to look at the top card of one of the piles, memorize it, and replace it, and the performer then gathers up the cards, placing the pile of which he knows the bottom card on top of the card which was selected. The chosen card can then be located by running through the deck until the memorized card is arrived at, when the spectator's card will be the next one to it toward the bottom of the pack.

If, by any chance, the spectator chooses the top card of the pile containing the card the performer has memorized, it will be necessary, in gathering up the cards, for him to glance quickly at the bottom card of one of the other piles and then place that pile on top of the chosen card. Experience proves, however, that this expedient will rarely have to be adopted.

THE BENT CARDS

ANOTHER excellent and simple method by which to locate a chosen card is as follows. The performer holds out the deck and allows a spectator to take a card. While he is noting it, the performer bends the remainder of the back by simply curving it over in his hand. When the chosen card is returned, it can easily be detected, as it will stand out slightly from the remainder of the pack.

A good way to reveal the chosen card when using this method is to place the deck behind your back and remove the chosen card in this position.

A SURPRISE FINISH

THIS is one of the most surprising methods of revealing a chosen card and is very easy to perform.

The magician first brings the chosen card to the top of the deck and then, after a few false shuffles, slides it around to the bottom of the deck. If the deck is held lengthwise in the right hand with the backs of the cards toward the palm, this movement can be executed very easily and inconspicuously by simply inserting the left fingertips between the deck and the palm of the right hand and calmly pulling the top card around to the bottom, where it arrives face up.

The performer then hands the pack to the person who chose the card and tells him to grasp it tightly between the thumb and fingertips of one hand, holding the thumb uppermost. When this is done, the performer strikes the deck a sharp downward blow, which causes all the cards to fall to the floor with the exception of the chosen one, which remains face up in the spectator's hand.

THE CARD IN THE HANDKERCHIEF

THIS is a very effective finish to a card trick and, though it requires a modicum of skill, it can be easily perfected with a few minutes' practice. The magician has one of the audience select a card, which is duly returned and shuffled into the deck. A gentleman's handkerchief is then borrowed, and the cards are placed in the center of it and wrapped up in its folds. The magician then holds the handkerchief aloft, and at his word of command the chosen card drops into sight from beneath the folds of the handkerchief.

The only difficult part of this trick is that of palming the chosen card from the top of the deck, but the slight movement necessary to effect this is easily covered up by a proper manipulation of the handkerchief. After the handkerchief has been borrowed, it should be placed on a table where it can readily be picked up. The deck is then placed in the left hand, the right hand is placed on top of it, and the chosen card, which has been previously brought to the top, is pushed quickly into the palm of the right hand by the left thumb. Retaining the card in place by slightly curving the fingers of the right hand, the performer at once picks up the handkerchief with his right hand and uses his left hand, which still holds the deck, to throw it over the palm of the right hand. If the handkerchief is placed conveniently, the entire process can be done almost instantaneously and the right hand concealing the chosen card will scarcely be exposed to the audience's sight.

The deck is next placed, face upward, in the center of the handkerchief, and the handkerchief is folded over it. The pack is then gripped by the right hand with the thumb on one side and the fingers on the other side, the pressure being sufficient to hold the chosen card, which is outside the handkerchief, in place. When the performer is ready to reveal the chosen card, he shakes the deck slightly and allows the card to drop down into sight, apparently coming from the midst of the deck.

TELLING WHICH CARD IS CUT

THE performer places a pack of cards on the palm of his left hand and asks one of the audience to cut the deck, placing the upper portion of the deck, that is, the cards that he removes in cutting, on the performer's palm beside the remainder of the deck. The performer then asks the spectator to remove the top card of the pile nearest to him and to note what card it is without telling anyone else. He then takes the top card of the other pile and explains that by looking at it he can immediately tell what card the spectator has, on account of the magnetic attraction between the cards. This proves to be the case, for as soon as he notes the card that he has picked up he names the card that the spectator is holding.

The secret of this trick is absurdly simple and consists in the performer's secretly noting the top card of the pack before commencing the trick. When the cards are cut, this card is on top of the pile nearest the spectator and is, of course, the one that he removes and that the performer names. Picking up the other card is simply a bit of mystification to throw the audience off the track, and it invariably makes them believe that the trick depends upon a previous arrangement of the cards. Hence, there is usually a request to do the trick again, and there is little danger in repeating it, for it has a way of becoming more mystifying each time it is done, owing to the audience looking for the secret in the wrong place.

It can easily be repeated indefinitely if the performer takes care to place the card he looks at, but does not show the audience, on top of the deck, when it will naturally be the card which the audience next "cuts" and removes. By the use of the false shuffle, the deck can be thoroughly shuffled to convince the audience that it is not arranged, yet the performer will always know the top card.

CATCHING A CHOSEN CARD

THIS is one of the best and most surprising ways to finish a card trick in which one of the spectators has chosen a card and returned it to the pack. After the cards have been shuffled, the performer throws them into the air, darts his hand among them, and snatches the chosen card from the midst of the falling deck.

This effect is obtained by getting the chosen card to the top of the deck by means of the pass and retaining it between the thumb and forefinger of the right hand when the cards are thrown in the air. The scattering of the cards prevents the audience from seeing it, and the performer apparently picks it out from the midst of the other cards as they are showering to the ground. The effect is considerably heightened if the performer makes a sudden lunge toward the cards, scattering them in all directions.

THE TRAVELING CARD

THE magician takes the top card from the deck, shows it to the audience, and places it in the center of the deck. He ruffles the cards and extends them toward the audience, requesting them to remove the top card. To their astonishment, it is the card that a moment before was placed in the center of the deck.

This very neat trick is accomplished by privately

removing the seven and eight of any suit from the deck and placing them on top of the deck with the eight beneath the seven. In doing the trick both cards are first removed from the top of the deck and held closely together so that they look like a single card. The audience believe, naturally, that they are being shown the eight alone. Both cards are then replaced, and the seven is removed and placed in the center of the deck, being turned toward the audience for a moment in order to let them see that it is the same card they were previously shown. No one will ever detect the slight difference between the seven and eight. The cards are then ruffled, the performer exclaims "Presto," and when the top card is removed it appears as if the eight had traveled back from the center to the top of the pack.

MIND READING WITH CARDS

A VERY effective and mystifying mind-reading trick can be done with three cards, the secret of which is so simple that it defies detection. The performer asks his audience to place three cards in a row face upward on the table and then tells them to choose any one of the three while he is absent from the room. Upon returning to the room, he immediately indicates the card which was selected.

This trick depends for its execution upon a confederate, who should preferably be a smoker. He, of course, remains in the room during the performer's absence and notes which of the three cards is chosen. As soon as it has been chosen, he indicates its position by the position of his cigar, cigarette, or pipe. If the chosen card is on the right end of the row, he places his cigarette in the right corner of his mouth; if it is the center card, he places it in the center of his mouth, and if it is the left-hand card he places it in the left corner of his mouth. The motions of smoking are so natural that nobody will notice any peculiarity in the confederate's movements, particularly if the performer is careful never to look at him until after he has looked at the cards and glanced at one or two other members of the group.

If there is no confederate handy who smokes, the chosen card's position can be just as easily indicated by a slight motion of the wrist. To indicate the right-hand card, he should bend his right wrist slightly outward and away from the body. If the center card, he should let his hand hang naturally down at his side, and if the left-hand card is chosen he should bend his wrist slightly in toward his body.

ANOTHER MIND-READING TRICK

THIS is another trick of the same nature as the one just described and may be preferred by some performers on account of the greater number of cards used and the heightened effect gained thereby.

Twenty-five cards are laid out on the table in five rows of five cards each. While the magician leaves the room, one of the cards is selected, and upon his return his confederate indicates it to him by means of a simple finger sign language. The fingers of the right hand stand for the five cross rows, the thumb indicating the top row, the forefinger the second row from the top, and so on. The fingers of the left hand are used to indicate the number of the chosen card in the cross row indicated by the right hand.

The confederate may either keep his hands closed, fold his arms, or let his hands hang naturally at his sides, depending upon his position in the room in relation to the performer. When he wishes to indicate a card, he simply extends the proper fingers of each hand, keeping his remaining fingers slightly closed. The movement should not be exaggerated enough to be generally noticeable, but just sufficient to catch the keen eye of the performer who, of course, is careful not to glance too promptly or for too long a time at his confederate.

CARD TELEPATHY

THIS is a very ingenious method of discovering what card a member of the audience has thought of.

Only twenty-one cards are used, and the performer deals these out face up on the table in three piles of seven cards each. He then asks a spectator to think of one of the cards and to tell him which pile it is in. He then gathers up the cards, placing the pile which contains the chosen card in the middle between the other two piles. The cards are dealt again in the same manner, and the performer again places the pile containing the chosen card in the middle as he gathers them up. When the cards are dealt the third time, the chosen card will be the fourth from the bottom in one of the piles and as soon as the spectator indicates the pile which contains it, the performer immediately picks it out and shows it to him, or else gathers the cards up and finishes the trick by revealing the card in some other way.

THE FIXED PACK

A FIXED pack, that is, one in which the cards are arranged according to a fixed system, or sequence, has the one drawback that it cannot be shuffled, but so many excellent tricks can be performed with such a pack that a description of one of the best methods of arrangement is given herewith.

The suits follow one another in the order of hearts, spades, diamonds, clubs, and the cards are arranged so that three numbers separate each card. Thus, starting with the three of hearts, the next card would be the six of spades, the next the nine of diamonds, the next the queen of clubs, and so on.

To do a mind-reading act with such a pack, the performer has one of the audience draw a card, and while he is looking at it, he tilts the upper portion of the deck and looks at the card next above the card selected. If he has an assistant, he shows this card to him. Anyone who knows how the cards are arranged can, of course, instantly tell which card was selected after he has once caught a glimpse of the card just above it.

THE NEW Q TRICK

THIS is a modern version of an old trick known as the "Q trick." The cards are spread out on the table in the shape of a Q, the majority of the cards forming a circle, and six or eight being appended like the tail of a Q. The performer then asks the audience to select a card by the following method: Start with the end card in the tail of the Q and count up the tail and around the left side of the circle as far as they wish. Then, calling the card at which they stop counting Number One, count back exactly the same number of cards, but instead of counting down the tail, continue on around the circle. Now the card at which they finally stop will be just as many cards distant from the tail and up the right side of the circle as there are cards in the tail.

While the audience are selecting their card the performer leaves the room, but as soon as the counting is completed he announces the card which has been selected. Before leaving the room, he counted up the right side of the circle himself and noted the card which would have to be selected, its position being predetermined by the number of cards in the tail. If the trick is repeated, the number of cards in the tail should be increased or diminished so that the same card will not be chosen a second time.

THE FIVE–PILE FORCE

THE performer holds a pack of cards face downward and, as he moves his hand across the table, drops a few cards at a time until there are five piles each containing approximately the same number of cards. He then asks a spectator to remove the top card of one of the end piles and place it on the next pile. Another card is removed from the end pile and placed on the second pile away, and two more cards are similarly taken from the end pile and placed on the remaining two piles. The spectator is then asked to look at the top card of the end pile and, after he has memorized it, to gather up the cards and shuffle them together. The performer then tells him the name of the card that he noted, or reveals it in some other way.

This is simply a mystifying method of forcing a card. Before commencing the trick, the performer opens out the cards in his hand with the faces toward him and notes the fifth card from the top. When the five piles have been made, he instructs the spectator to remove the cards from the pile which was previously the top of the deck. Thus, when four cards are taken off and placed on the four other piles, the card on top of the fifth pile is the card that was originally the fifth from the top of the deck and that the performer memorized before the trick began.

CARD JUGGLING

A VERY pretty effect can be obtained by balancing a card on the back of the fingers, and when this little flourish is unexpectedly shown in the interval between two other tricks it is very surprising.

It is accomplished by secretly gripping a pin or needle between the knuckles of the third and fourth fingers and resting the card lightly against it. A few minutes' practice will show just how to place the pin and the best angle at which to rest the card. It must be done deftly, but, if thoroughly practised, will prove very mystifying.

CARD BALANCED ON A GLASS

ANOTHER little juggling feat that can be introduced as a bit of by-play is to balance a drinking glass on the edge of a playing card. It is accomplished by pushing the middle finger of the hand that is holding the card up to the top edge of the card and resting the glass upon the end of the finger. The other hand should be employed in making mesmeric passes over the glass, and the glass should ultimately be allowed to fall, as this confirms the impression that it was actually being balanced on the card alone.

CARD DISAPPEARING FROM THE PACK

ONE of the audience selects a card, which is then returned and the pack shuffled. The performer turns the cards face up and deals them onto the table, but the chosen card has mysteriously disappeared and is not in the pack.

The beauty of this trick is that it is all done before the audience begins to look for any fast moves or suspicious actions on the part of the performer. It is done as follows: Just as soon as the spectator has chosen his card, the performer moistens the first and second fingers of his right hand with his tongue. He then cuts the deck and thoroughly moistens the top card of the lower half of the deck. This movement may be hidden by turning away under the pretense of not wishing accidentally to catch a glimpse of the chosen card. Still holding the cards as cut, the performer extends the deck toward the spectator, who puts his card between the two halves of the deck and so directly on top of the moistened card. Before shuffling, the performer gives the pack two or three firm squeezes and the chosen card will then stick fast to the card beneath it even though the pack is thoroughly shuffled.

IMPROMPTU RISING–CARD TRICK

THIS is a new version of the old rising-card trick and can be performed without apparatus of any nature. A card is chosen and returned, and the deck is shuffled. The performer then takes the cards in his left hand and holds them with their faces toward the audience. Extending his right forefinger, he places it on top of the deck and raises and lowers it several times. No card rises from the pack during these first attempts, but at last the chosen card adheres to the forefinger and follows it steadily upward and out of the pack.

The explanation is simplicity itself. The card is first brought to the top by means of the pass, and the deck is then held in the performer's left hand directly in front of his body, and the right hand with the forefinger extended is placed right in back of the deck. To lift the chosen card, the performer merely extends his right little finger until it touches the chosen card, and then, when the forefinger is raised, the little finger pushes the card up at the same time.

THE FOUR–ACE TRICK

THERE are many versions of the four-ace trick, but the one here described is the simplest to execute and accomplishes the same result as the others—namely, to separate the four aces and then bring them magically together.

The aces are taken from the deck and handed to one of the spectators. "Now, put one on top," says the performer, "and another one on the bottom." This is done, and the performer then asks casually, "And what two aces have you left?" The spectator looks down at the cards in his hands, and as he does so the performer cuts the pack, which he is holding face down in his left hand, grasps the lower section between the fingers and thumb of his right hand, and brings it out to the left and from beneath the top section, which is allowed to fall into the palm of the left hand. It looks as though the pack had merely been cut in the ordinary manner.

The two remaining aces are then placed on top of the lower half of the pack, which brings them on top of the ace which was previously put on top of the deck. Then, when the upper half of the pack which, before the trick cut was made, was the lower half, is replaced, all four aces will be together in the center of the pack.

ANOTHER FOUR-ACE TRICK

THIS trick requires a little address to perform effectively, but, as with every trick in the book, *if it is practised* until the performer is sure of himself, it will mystify any audience, no matter how observant or critical. The four aces are removed from the deck, shown to the audience, and replaced on top of the pack. They are then dealt face downward on the table in a row, and three indifferent cards are dealt on top of each. Presto! The aces are magically gathered together into one pile.

When the aces have been removed and are being shown to the audience, the performer puts his little finger in the center of the deck and turns the lower half face upward, so that the two halves of the deck are facing each other. The aces are then returned and placed on top of the deck, and one of them is dealt off onto the table, the performer showing it casually to the audience as he puts it down so that they can see it is really an ace and that no substitution has been made. Now the pack must be turned over, and in order to direct attention away from the cards the performer should introduce a little patter, telling the audience that his intention is to put the four aces on the table, cover them with other cards, etc. While he is talking, he turns the pack over and then deals three indifferent cards onto the table beside the ace. The pack is then turned back to its original position, the three remaining aces are dealt off on top of the first one, and the three other cards are each covered with three cards. The aces are now all together in one pile, and their marvelous flight can be revealed at the performer's pleasure.

CALLING THE CARDS

THIS trick is most effective when presented as an experiment in hypnotic control, a demonstration of the performer's magic will which forces the audience to do its bidding.

The pack is spread face down on the table, and the performer calls for five cards, one at a time. As he calls the name of each card, one of the spectators draws a card from the pack and hands it to the performer, while another spectator writes down the name of the card. As soon as the fifth card has been drawn, the five cards are thrown face up on the table and are found to be identical with the five that the performer called for and that were written down.

Before commencing the trick, the performer takes a card, say the ace of hearts, from the deck and conceals it in the palm of his left hand. The deck is then spread on the table, and the performer calls for the ace of hearts. A spectator draws a card at random and hands it to the performer face downward. The performer looks at it casually as though verifying it, and notes that it is, for example, the six of clubs. He then calls for the six of clubs, receives another card, calls for it, and so on until five cards have been drawn. The fifth card is placed in back of the ace of hearts and retained in the palm of the left hand while the other five cards are passed to the right hand and thrown on the table. While the audience are checking the cards against the list, the performer picks up the pack and replaces the palmed card.

There is another method of doing this trick which obviates palming. The performer memorizes the sixth card from the top of the deck. He then indicates what cards the spectator is to hand him by touching them, the last card he touches being the one he has memorized.

THE MASTER CUT

THE cards are shuffled and the performer then cuts the deck at any point designated by the audience. The performer then lifts the upper portion of the deck so that the audience can see the bottom card, but does not look at the card himself. He then hands the deck to a spectator to shuffle, and when it is returned he instantly finds the card that the audience saw, drawing it from the pack held behind his back, naming it, or producing it in some other way.

The secret of this trick is one that can be used in a variety of combinations. It is known as the "bent card." When the upper portion of the deck is being replaced after the cut, the performer pushes the bottom card down a half an inch or so, so that when the two parts of the deck are reunited the bottom card projects behind the others. With his right thumb he then bends up the left corner of the card and at once pushes it back into the deck. Now, no matter how thoroughly the cards are shuffled, he can always locate the bent card either by sight or by touch.

THE OBEDIENT CARD

A CARD is drawn from the pack by one of the audience, returned, and shuffled into the pack. Three spectators are asked to call any number less than ten, and when they have done so the numbers are totaled and the performer announces that he will make the chosen card appear at that number from the top of the deck. He counts off the proper number, but the last card turned up is not the chosen one. Apparently something has gone wrong, but the performer hands the deck to a spectator and asks him to count off the number of cards determined upon. The last card counted by the spectator is the chosen one.

The chosen card is brought to the top of the deck as explained above and retained there by the false shuffle. When the number has been decided, which is, say, twelve, the performer counts off twelve cards, and, of course, the twelfth card is not the chosen one.

He then puts the twelve cards on top of the deck and hands it to a spectator. Now the chosen card is the twelfth from the top, since it is the bottom card of the twelve that the performer counted off.

THE SVENGALI CARD TRICK

THE performer deals seven cards face up on the table and asks a member of the audience mentally to select one of them and to think of it with deep concentration. When the spectator has indicated that he is thinking of his card, the performer writes something on a piece of paper and seals the paper in an envelope which he places in his pocket. The performer then asks which was the chosen card, and upon being told he burns it and throws the ashes into the air. The envelope is then taken from his pocket and handed to a spectator, who opens it and finds the name of the chosen card written on the piece of paper inside.

Prior to the performance the magician writes the names of six cards on small pieces of paper, which he encloses in envelopes and puts in his pocket, arranged in order so that he can instantly pick out whichever one he wishes. The six cards whose names he has written down are placed on top of the pack, and one other card is placed with them. The seventh card is the one whose name the performer writes on a piece of paper in front of the audience. As soon as the spectator has named his card, the performer can, of course, pick out the proper envelope.

It is not necessary to burn the card, though this is the method used by most professionals. Instead, the seven cards can be gathered up and shuffled back into the deck; the performer then exclaims: "Presto!" and the magic word will be sufficient to do the trick.

THE CARDS FROM THE POCKET

THE cards are thoroughly shuffled by the audience and placed in the performer's inside coat pocket. The audience then calls the names of various cards, and the performer instantly reaches into his pocket and produces the card called for.

Two packs of cards with the same markings on the back are required for this trick. One pack is divided into four packets, each packet consisting of all the cards of one suit arranged in order from ace to king. One of these packets is placed in the right lower waistcoat pocket, one in the right upper waistcoat pocket, one is tucked between the belt and the body on the performer's right side, and one is encircled with a rubber band and placed in the inside coat pocket. All four packets are thus readily accessible, and, with a little practice, any card called for can be picked out in a matter of seconds.

INSTANT CARD READING

THE cards are shuffled and returned to the performer, who fans them out and holds them before one of the spectators, the cards being held vertically and with the faces toward the audience. The spectator is asked to touch one of the cards with his finger, and no sooner has he done so than the performer tells him what card it is. No matter how often the trick is repeated, the performer never fails to name the right card.

When the spectator touches a card, the performer quietly turns up its left bottom corner with his right thumb, thus permitting him to see the index number and suit. If practised carefully, the trick is absolutely undetectable.

THE YOGI WONDER–CARD TRICK

THIS is a new trick, whose effect is so mysterious that only a yogi, or one with supernatural powers, could seemingly do it. The performer deals five piles of four cards each onto the table, places each pile in a separate envelope, and gives the envelopes to five members of the audience with the request that each person mentally select one of the cards given him. When this has been done the performer takes another deck and deals off five cards at a time, showing each group of five to the audience and requesting them to indicate when they see one of the cards that has been selected. The performer then instantly tells them which card is being thought of.

To do this trick the cards must be arranged before the performance. Five groups of four cards each are made up and placed on top of one deck. The performer mentally numbers these groups from one to five and distributes them, say, from left to right, so that he can easily remember which person has which group.

These same twenty cards are then removed from another deck and arranged in four piles of five cards each, each pile containing one card from each of the first five groups. The first cards of each group are put together in one pile, the first card of Number One group being placed on the bottom face up, the first card of Number Two group on top of it, and so on. The next pile contains the second cards of each of the first groups similarly arranged, and the other two piles are made up of the third and fourth cards.

These piles are placed in the second deck, so that five or ten other cards separate them from each other. It is best to put five indifferent cards on top of the deck, so that none of the audience's cards will be among the first five dealt off, thus creating the impression that the cards are not arranged.

Now, if a spectator says his card is among those the performer has in his hand, the performer notes what group of four cards that person was given. It is, say, Number Three, so the card thought of will be the third from the bottom of the five cards the performer is holding. This trick requires a little study, but the effect is well worth it, and, once learned, it will be one of the best in the magician's repertoire.

THE KINGS AND SEVENS

THE four kings and the four sevens are removed from the pack and shown to the audience. The kings are then placed in one person's pocket and the sevens in another person's. At the magic word of command the cards mysteriously change places.

Apparently, great sleight of hand is needed to change the position of the cards unobserved, but in reality this trick requires no deftness at all. Before showing the trick, the performer removes the four eights and places them on top of the deck. In doing the trick, he first looks through the deck and picks out the kings and sevens, which he shows to the audience and casually replaces on top of the deck, the kings first and the sevens on top. Then, as though not sure that everybody has seen the cards, he removes them again, this time removing the eights as well and concealing the sevens behind the kings. The eights should be held so that the lower of the two center pips of the front card is covered by the fingers, thus making it look like a seven. The lower pips on the other eights will be hidden by the front card so that they will likewise appear to be sevens.

Now replace the cards on top of the deck, the eights first, then the kings, and on top of all the sevens. The audience supposes that the kings are on top and the sevens beneath them, but they are really in just the opposite order. Deal off the sevens and put them in a spectator's pocket, telling him that they are the kings, which, of course, he has no reason to doubt. Deal off the kings and put them in another person's pocket, telling him that they are sevens. Then give the cards the magic command to change places, and, as far as the audience is concerned, they will appear to do so.

TELLING WHAT CARD IS THOUGHT OF

AFTER the pack has been shuffled, the performer deals off four cards and hands them to a spectator with the request that he remember any one of them. Four more cards are given to each of three other spectators with the same request. When all sixteen cards have been returned, the performer deals them out on the table in four heaps and when told by the spectators which heaps contain their cards, he instantly tells them what cards they are thinking of.

When the first person has thought of his card, the performer takes back his cards and places them face downward on the table. The second person's are put

on top of them, then the third and fourth persons.'
The cards are then dealt out face downward in four
heaps. The first person's card will be the uppermost
in the heap he names, the second person's card will be
the second from the top in the heap named, and so on.
The trick can also be done with three people by giving them three cards apiece.

THE REVERSED CARD

THE magician places four kings in a row on the
table and asks the audience to turn one of them
around while he leaves the room. Upon his return,
he immediately tells which of the cards has been
turned around.

This trick depends upon a little known peculiarity
of the court cards in any deck; namely, that the
white margins at one end are almost always a little
narrower than those at the opposite end. If the four
kings are placed so that the wide margins all face one
way, the reversed card can be detected instantly by
noting the margins and comparing them.

THE SUSPENDED CARDS

THE magician places a number of cards on the
palm of his hand, subjects them to a few hypnotic passes, and inverts his hand. Instead of falling to
the floor, all the cards remain magically suspended

to his hand, and he walks about through the audience to show them that there are no threads or other visible means of support.

One card is prepared before the performance by fastening to its back a small piece of flesh-colored court plaster or adhesive tape bent to form a tab. This card is the first one the performer places on his palm, and the other cards are tucked in beneath it, the tab being gripped between the fingers.

THE TORN-CORNER CARD

THERE have been several methods in vogue of accomplishing this famous trick, but one and all have required the use of rather elaborate apparatus, mechanical cards, etc. The method here described is the best, by all odds, for amateur work, being quickly prepared for and requiring only the simplest sleight of hand.

In effect, a member of the audience is requested to name any card in the deck. The performer removes this card and gives it to the spectator to tear up. The pieces are collected on a plate, and the performer picks a piece at random and returns it to the spectator. The rest of the torn pieces are then placed in an envelope, the performer says a few magic words, opens the envelope, and removes the card, which is wholly restored with the exception of one corner. When the card is given to the spectator, it is found that the piece he is holding exactly fits in the torn corner.

The performer prepares for the trick by arranging two packs of cards with similar backs, placing the two cards of the same denomination from each pack together in the double pack. Thus the two aces of each suit are next each other, the two twos are together, and so on. When the spectator names a card, the performer runs through the double deck and picks it out, at the same time placing his little finger just above its duplicate. On his way back to the table to get the plate for the torn pieces, he slips the duplicate card to the top of the deck and tears off one corner, retaining it in his right hand.

When the torn pieces have been placed on the plate, the performer starts to walk back to his table, but stops as though he had suddenly remembered something, returns to the spectator, and hands him the corner of the duplicate card, pretending to pick it up at random from the plate. He then returns to his table and picks up an envelope which has been prepared so as to have a double compartment inside. This is done by cutting off the back of another envelope and fitting it inside the first one. Into one compartment of this envelope he pours the torn pieces, and into the other compartment he slips the duplicate card from which the corner has been torn. Presto! The envelope is opened and the duplicate card is removed, the performer holding up the envelope so that the audience can look inside it and see that the pieces have disappeared. The trick is concluded by allowing the spectator to fit the piece he is holding onto the corner of the torn card.

THE ONE, TWO, THREE CARD TRICK

THREE aces, three twos, and three threes are removed from a pack of cards and placed on the table face downward in three piles, one pile containing the aces, one the twos, and one the threes. One of the spectators is asked to pick up one of the piles and place it on top of another, and then to place the remaining pile on top of the other two. The cards are then cut as often as the audience desires and returned to the performer, who deals them out in three piles, making the top card the bottom one of the first pile, the second card the bottom one of the second pile, the third card the bottom one of the third pile, then placing the fourth card on top of the first one, and so on.

The audience is asked to choose a pile and the performer picks it up and shows that one of each kind of card, an ace, a two, and a three have been gathered together in it. The trick is repeated, and whichever pile the audience chooses is found to contain one of each card.

The trick works itself, and if the steps outlined above are followed, each of the final piles will invariably contain an ace, a two, and a three. The performer should see that the cards are only cut singly each time; that is, some of the top cards are removed and placed on the table and the remaining cards are placed on top of them. If this is done, the trick cannot go wrong.

THE CUT CARD

THE performer gives one of the spectators a sealed envelope and then places a pack of cards on the table. Another spectator is asked to cut the cards at any point he wishes and the first spectator then places the envelope between the two halves of the deck. A moment elapses while the performer makes a mystic pass and murmurs a magic word. The envelope is then removed and opened, and is found to contain a piece of paper on which is written the name of a card, say the ten of clubs. Upon turning over the card just beneath the envelope, it is found to be the ten of clubs.

The trick is accomplished by means of an extremely clever ruse which, despite its apparent openness, never fails to work. Before showing the trick the performer writes the name of a card on a piece of paper which he seals in an envelope. This card is then placed on the top of the deck. When the deck is cut, the top card will be on top of one of the halves and the envelope is boldly placed on the top card, the other half of the deck being replaced on top of all. Thus the card just beneath the envelope is bound to be the one whose name is written on the piece of paper in the envelope.

THE REVERSED PACK

AN ORDINARY pack of cards can be so arranged that, without the use of sleight of hand, the performer can instantly locate cards that have been drawn and returned by members of the audience.

Certain cards are reversible, that is, the pips are printed or arranged so that if the cards are turned around, the change in position can be noted at once. These cards are the ace, three, five, six, seven, eight, and nine of clubs, hearts, and spades, and the seven of diamonds.

A pack is made up that consists only of these cards. all of which are arranged to point in one direction. After one or more spectators have drawn a card, the performer reverses the pack. Thus, when the spectators return their cards, they will be upside down in relation to the other cards and can be detected at once by glancing quickly through the pack.

FINDING A CHOSEN CARD

ONE of the simplest methods of finding a chosen card is as follows. Sixteen cards are used which are laid out on the table in four rows of four cards each. The performer asks one of the spectators to think of one of the cards and to tell him in which horizontal row it lies.

The cards are now gathered up in packs of four, care being taken to have the fourth, or bottom, card of each pack one of the cards which was in the horizontal row designated by the spectator. Thus, the spectator's card will be either the fourth, eighth, twelfth, or sixteenth card in the pack as it lies in the performer's hand.

Now the cards are laid out again, the first four being placed in a horizontal row, the second four in another horizontal row just beneath them, and so on. The spectator's card will now be one of the four cards on the right-hand end of the four rows. The performer asks him to point out which horizontal row it is in, and he immediately knows the card, for it is the one on the right-hand end of the row designated.

THE MAGICIAN'S CHOICE

EVERY magician should know this method of revealing a chosen card, for it can be used in a variety of combinations and will often come in handy.

Suppose a card has been chosen and brought to the top of the deck. The four top cards are laid out on the table separately, and the magician asks the audience to point out any two of them. If one of the cards pointed out is the chosen card, he picks up the other two, saying: "Very well; we will leave the two cards you have chosen." If, however, the chosen card is one of the two which were not designated, the magician calmly removes the two which were pointed out, saying: "Very well; we will remove the cards you have chosen." In either case, the chosen card is left on the table.

The audience are then asked to designate one of the two remaining cards. If they point out the chosen card, it is turned over at once; but if they point out the other card, the magician calmly picks it up and requests the audience to turn over the card left on the table, which is, of course, the chosen one.

THE HIDDEN TOTAL

FOR the mathematically inclined this trick will prove extremely interesting as well as puzzling, for they will not be able to understand how it works. The performer requests the audience to shuffle a pack of cards and place them in piles on the table, as described below. He leaves the room while this is being done, but upon his return immediately announces the total of the cards on the bottom of the piles.

In arranging the cards, one is first placed on the table and sufficient cards to total 12 are placed on top of it, adding the number of cards added to the number on the first card. Thus if the first card were a 4, 8 cards would be put on top of it; if it were a 7, 5 cards would be added; if a 10, 2 cards, and so on. The face cards are always counted as tens. When one pile is completed, another and another are made in the same way until all the cards have been used. If there are a few cards left over, as is generally the case, they are placed in a separate pile.

To calculate the total of the bottom cards, the performer counts 13 for each pile in excess of 4 piles, and adds the number of left-over cards to the product. If there are 10 piles and 6 cards left over, for example, the performer subtracts 4 from 10, leaving 6, and multiplies 13 by 6, giving 78. To this he adds 6 (the number of left-over cards) which makes 84, and this is the correct total of the bottom cards.

A GREAT MIND-READING TRICK

THIS is one of the most baffling of all card tricks, yet it can be performed at a moment's notice provided you have an assistant who already knows the trick. If not, one of the group present may be made a confidant and taught the secret in a few seconds.

While the assistant leaves the room, the spectators select a card from the pack, memorize it, and return it. The cards are then placed face down on the table and the assistant returns and instantly tells what card was chosen.

The assistant is able to tell the card by the position in which the performer places the pack on the table. The table is mentally divided into twelve squares representing the twelve cards from the ace to the queen. The ace is represented by the left-hand outer corner, the deuce by the square next to it toward the right, the three by the next square to the right, and the four by the square formed at the right-hand outer corner. The center of the table is likewise divided into four squares representing the five, six, seven, and eight, and the inner side of the table is given over to the nine, ten, jack, and queen. To show the assistant that a king was chosen, the pack is not squared up before being placed on the table, but is put down anywhere *disarranged*.

The suit of the card is shown by the direction in which the pack points. To indicate clubs it is placed so as to point to one side of the table. To indicate hearts it is pointed toward the left-hand outer corner. To indicate spades it is placed at right angles to the position used to show clubs, and to indicate diamonds it is pointed toward the right-hand outer corner.

THE CARD FROM THE POCKET

A DECK of cards is thoroughly shuffled, and the magician proceeds to pick out five cards at random, naming each card as he draws it from the pack. One of the spectators is requested to think of one of the cards, not telling anyone which card he selects. The pack is then placed in the performer's inside coat pocket, after being thoroughly shuffled by the audience. The spectator is then asked to name his card, and the magician instantly reaches into his pocket and draws it out of the pack.

The secret of this exceedingly mystifying trick is as simple as the effect is profound. Before the performance the magician memorizes five cards and places them, arranged so that he can pick any one of them at will, in his right upper vest pocket. When he draws the five cards from the deck, he does not give the names of the cards he actually takes, but gives instead the names of the five cards in his pocket. When the spectator names the card he has thought of, the magician reaches into his vest pocket and withdraws it, though it appears to the audience as if he reached into his inside coat pocket in which the balance of the pack has been placed. There is no doubt but that this is one of the best card tricks that can be done without the use of sleight of hand. Try it and you will see.

AN INDETECTABLE CARD TRICK

THE cards are thoroughly shuffled and placed face downward on the table. Turning his back, the magician asks one of the spectators to count any number of cards between two and twelve from the top of the pack, laying them face down on the table.

The names of these cards are then written on a piece of paper so that they can be remembered.

Another spectator is then asked to place the balance of the deck on top of the chosen cards and to give the pack as many cuts as he wishes. Turning around, the performer looks through the cards and at once tells how many were counted off and what their names are.

The performer does this trick by noting the top and bottom cards just before he places the deck on the table and turns his back. In giving his instructions, he is careful to tell the spectator to lay the cards face downward on the table in the order in which they are lifted off the deck—that is, the top card first, the second card next, and so on. Thus, when the balance of the deck is placed on top of the cards that have been counted off, the former top card will be on the bottom of the deck, the chosen cards will be on top of it, and the former bottom card comes next. No matter how many times the deck is given a single cut, the order will not be disturbed, and all the performer has to do is to locate the cards that were on the top and bottom of the deck at the beginning of the trick and name the cards that are in between them, including the top card but excluding the bottom card.

TRICKS WITH MATCHES

THE LIGHTNING MATCH VANISH

MATCHES have an advantage over many of the other objects that a magician uses, in that they can be completely vanished in the twinkling of an eye and the hand shown to be absolutely empty, whereas most other objects must be palmed in such a way that the hand can be only partially shown.

In vanishing matches, they are tucked in behind a ring worn on the third finger of the right hand. The matches are taken one at a time between the thumb and forefinger of the right hand and the hand is tossed in the air as though throwing the match away. Under cover of this motion the third and fourth fingers are bent in and the match is slipped under the ring at the back of the finger. This is a trick that should be practised assiduously, as frequent occasions for showing it are sure to be presented, and the magician will find it a very effective impromptu demonstration of his powers.

TWO FROM ONE

A SINGLE match is exhibited, and the performer shows that his hands are otherwise empty and there is nothing up his sleeve. Holding the match well away from his body, he waves his hand through the air, and there are suddenly two matches instead of one.

This beautiful experiment in magical multiplication is accomplished by using a single match, which has been carefully split in two halves with a sharp knife. The two halves are put together and exhibited to the audience as being a perfectly ordinary match. When the hand is waved in the air, the halves are separated, and at a very short distance it will be impossible to tell that they are not two whole matches.

THE BOX OF LIGHTED MATCHES

IT IS quite startling to see a lighted match drawn from an ordinary match box, and the magician can surprise his friends considerably by performing this feat unexpectedly.

The match box used must be prepared by pasting on the inside of one end of the cover a small piece cut from the side of another match box. The drawer full of matches is then pushed into the cover with the heads at the opposite end to that on which the piece of the other box has been glued. In producing a lighted match, the magician opens the box so that the blank ends of the matches are showing, and as he withdraws one, he presses down on the blank end so that the head is forced against the inside of the cover, thus lighting it just before it comes clear of the box.

THE BALANCED MATCH

THE performer asks if anybody in the audience is able to balance a match upright on the table, and though some of them may try, they will be unable to accomplish the feat. Taking the same match that they have been using, the performer at once balances it on one end.

While the spectators are trying their luck, the performer secretly moistens his right thumb and forefinger. When he picks up the match he does so with these fingers and rolls it between them in order to moisten the bottom end. With a pretense of great care he stands it on the table and presses down firmly, and when his hand is removed the match stays in an upright position.

THE HYPNOTIZED MATCH BOX

THE real effectiveness of this little trick is not usually appreciated until it has been tried out on an audience, when its true worth as a bit of magical by-play will be realized.

The magician places a match box on his outstretched palm and makes several hypnotic passes over it. Slowly it rises until it is standing on end. The hand is turned sideways and upside down, yet the match box still clings to it. At any time it can be removed and passed for examination.

In placing the box on his palm the magician opens the drawer slightly and closes it upon the loose skin at the base of his fingers, the box being held upside down. Now, when the fingers are straightened out, the box will mysteriously rise until it is standing on end and the hand can be turned any way without its falling off.

The same effect can also be obtained by placing the box on the back of the wrist.

THE FULL AND EMPTY MATCH BOX

WHEN someone asks him for a match, the magician finds that his box is empty, but by simply murmuring a magic word over it, it is magically filled with matches.

This effective little apparatus can be made in a few minutes. Remove the lable from one match box and paste it on the bottom of another, so that both top and bottom of the second box are identical. Then wedge as many matches as possible between the bottom of the drawer and the bottom of the box, breaking down the bottom so that the matches will lie flush with the sides of the drawer. If neatly done, the false layer of matches will pass muster for a full box except when examined very closely. By turning the box around in the hand, it can be made to appear empty or full, at the magician's pleasure.

When using the match box it is a good scheme to

tell your audience that the trick is done by substitution and that two match boxes are really used. In their efforts to catch sight of the second box, they will forget the possibility of there being only one box.

THE NEW FULL AND EMPTY MATCH BOX

IF ANYONE in the audience suspects that the box used in the previous trick is prepared in some way or other, and asks to examine it, the magician can concede his request by the use of another box which he has ready in his pocket for just such an emergency.

This box is entirely empty, but the top of one end of the drawer has been cut down just a little more than the thickness of a match. The bottom is cut from another match box and a layer of matches is glued to it. A piece of elastic is then fastened to the end of this false layer, and a safety pin is attached to the other end of the elastic. The box, with the false layer in place, is carried in the right-hand vest pocket, the safety pin being pinned into the back of the waistcoat.

If the trick is performed as a sequel to the previous one, the first match box should be placed in the left vest pocket and the one just described should be withdrawn from the right pocket, the movement being made to appear as though the original box were being withdrawn. It is opened and shown to be full, the performer keeping the false layer of matches in place with his thumb. The box is closed, the thumb withdrawn, and the elastic immediately snaps the matches out of sight, whereupon the box is shown empty and passed for examination.

MATERIALIZING MATCHES

THIS is still another way to confound your critics, who think that a prepared match box is necessary in order to make matches appear and disappear. The magician shows a match box to be empty, closes it, and immediately it is opened by one of the audience and found to contain a number of matches.

The matches are concealed all the time between one end of the drawer and the inside of the box cover. As many as possible are wedged into this hiding place, and the drawer is then pushed through the box and halfway out the other side, so that the box is half open. In closing it, the right thumb pushes against the ends of the matches, forcing them into the drawer.

SAWING THROUGH A MATCH BOX

THE performer produces a match box and a playing card, and using the card as a saw, proceeds to cut right through the box, matches and all. When the card has cut through to the bottom of the box, the drawer, which is full of matches, is pushed back and forth, the matches and drawer apparently passing right through the card.

The match box is prepared prior to the performance by cutting away the center portion of each side of the drawer. A block of wood is then glued in each end of the drawer and a layer or two of match ends is glued on top of the blocks, the heads at one end and the bottoms at the other end. The cover of the box is prepared by slitting the top crossways and continuing the slit down both sides, thus making a groove for the card to fit in.

In executing the trick the performer pretends to exert considerable effort in forcing the card through the box, thus adding to the realism of the effect. The drawer is then pushed to and fro, showing it to be apparently full of matches. At the conclusion of the trick the performer hands the card to the audience, puts the match box in his pocket, and immediately withdraws another unprepared match box, which he hands for examination.

MATCH–BOX MONTE

HERE is a new version of the "pick-the-ace" trick, which will keep the audience guessing. Three match boxes, one of which is half full and the other two empty, are placed on the table. The magician shifts them around, shaking the half-full box occasionally to give the audience a clue, yet they are never able to pick it out from the empty boxes and always pick an empty box.

The secret lies in the fact that the performer has secretly concealed a second half-full match box up his right sleeve, holding it in place with a rubber band. When he has the other half-full box in his hand, he never shakes it; but when he is shifting either of the empty boxes, he can give it a shake and the matches in the box up his sleeve will rattle. With clever handling, this trick will cause endless fun and mystification.

THE MYSTIC MATCHES

THE performer takes several matches and breaks them into six pieces, each about half an inch long. These are placed on the table, and the performer picks up five of them, one at a time, with his right hand and places them in his left hand. He then picks up the sixth piece and places it in his pocket. The left hand is immediately opened, and the sixth piece is found to have flown into it, for there are now six pieces in the left hand.

In breaking up the matches, the performer really makes *seven* pieces, and one of these he conceals between the base of the second and third fingers of his right hand. When dropping the fifth piece into his left hand, he releases this extra piece and allows it to fall into his left hand at the same time.

If the trick is to be repeated, the sixth piece, which

is ostensibly put in the pocket, should be retained in the right hand and concealed between the fingers until the time arrives to drop it into the left hand.

THE BROKEN MATCH

A MATCH is borrowed from one of the audience, thus proving that it is unprepared in any way, and is folded up in a handkerchief. One or more of the spectators are then requested to break the match through the folds of the handkerchief, yet, when it is unfolded, the match is found to be perfectly whole, having been miraculously restored.

Prior to the performance, the magician has secretly inserted a match of his own in the hem of the handkerchief he proposes to use, and it is this match that the audience unwittingly breaks.

THE MAGNETIC MATCH BOX

IT IS well known that, if you put anything against the vertical wall of a room and do not fasten it there, it will immediately fall to the ground, yet this little experiment proves that the magician can defy the laws of gravity at will and accomplish the above-stated impossibility with ease.

A safety match box is placed against a door and adheres to it without support of any kind. The trick is accomplished by pressing the match box very firmly against the door, at the same time pushing it upward an inch or so. If this is done, the box will adhere to the wood for an indefinite length of time. The same effect can be obtained by using a pencil instead of a match box.

THE HEADS–UP MATCH BOX

THE magician takes a box of safety matches in his hand and throws it into the air. It lands on the table with the label side up. Attention is drawn to this fact, and the performer throws the box again, and as often as desired, always making it land with the label side up.

The secret of this mystifying little trick lies in the fact that the performer has concealed a half dollar between the bottom of the drawer and the outside shell of the match box. The weight of the coin will always turn the box over and make it fall right side up.

THE MATCH TRIANGLES

HOW is it possible to arrange six matches so that they will form four equilateral triangles of the same size? The average person will find it an impossibility and will have to be shown how to do it by the magician who has proposed the problem.

The diagram makes the solution of the problem clear. Three matches are laid on the table in the form

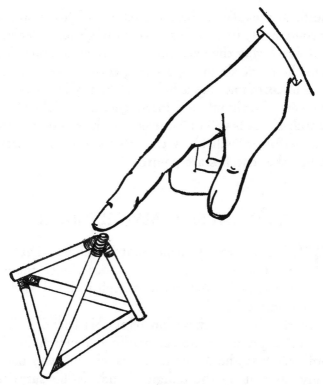

of a triangle, and the other three are arranged in pyramidal shape above them. There are thus four exactly identical triangles.

SEEING THROUGH A MATCH BOX

THIS is one of the simplest tricks imaginable, but it never fails to mystify. A match box is borrowed from some member of the audience, and the performer explains that, by reason of his power of second sight, he is able to see through its cover and tell which way the heads of the matches are pointing. This he proceeds to do, proving correct every time.

If a box of matches is held very lightly in the center between the thumb and forefinger, the weight of the matches' heads will pull one end of the box down, and the performer will know that this is the end toward which the matches are pointing.

TWO AMUSING MATCH TRICKS

THESE are two amusing match sleights that will be found useful on various occasions, though they are scarcely important enough to be classed as "programme" tricks.

In the first the magician offers his friend a light for his cigar or cigarette. Striking a match in the ordinary way, he hands it to his victim, who naturally takes it by the unlighted end. To his surprise, he has nothing but a half a match stick and no light at all, for before handing the match to him, the magician broke it in two between his fingers, and in offering it to him, retained the lighted end, with which he calmly proceeds to light his own cigarette.

The second trick is an experiment in long-distance blowing. Lighting a match, the magician holds it in his right fingertips with his right arm outstretched. Then, crooking his left arm, he blows down his left coat sleeve. Apparently the air travels down his coat sleeve, across his back, and out the other coat sleeve, for the match is instantly blown out.

To extinguish a match in this way, it is held between the thumb and the tip of the first finger. At the same instant that the magician blows down his left coat sleeve, thus directing attention to that quarter, he gives the match a quick snap with his right middle finger. The nail of the middle finger catches the match and draws it backward about a quarter of an inch and then suddenly releases it, thus giving the match a little fillip which is just sufficient to extinguish it.

THE MULTIPLYING MATCH BOX

WHEN performed on the professional stage this trick is accomplished by means of quite difficult sleight of hand, but the method here described requires practically no skill and is every bit as effective. The performer exhibits a match box which he holds in his fingertips. Showing his other hand to be empty, he passes it over the box, which is instantly changed to two boxes. Once more the hand is passed over, and a third match box makes its appearance.

The two extra match boxes are concealed inside the one first shown to the audience. It consists of the shell of an ordinary box in one end of which is glued the end of a drawer, so that, when this end is shown the audience, the box looks perfectly natural and un-prepared. The opposite end is left open. The second match box is made from the drawer of the original box by cutting down the sides slightly and pasting a top and sides on it. One end of this second box is cut away entirely so that the third box can be slid in and out. The third box is made in the same way as the second, but is cut down all around so that it will fit easily inside the second one.

In showing the trick, the first box, containing the other two, is exhibited at the right fingertips, the open ends being downward. Under cover of the left hand, the hidden boxes are dropped into the palm of the hand and brought to the right fingertips with the aid of the left thumb, which pushes them upward. The second and third boxes are shown as one, and the third box is subsequently produced in the same manner as before.

MATCHSTICK MATHEMATICS

THIS is one of the simplest tricks imaginable, but it is one that is very seldom detected. The performer gives a spectator a box of matches and asks him to remove any number he pleases under, say, twenty. When he has done so, the performer takes some matches himself and says, "Now I have as many matches as you have, enough more to make twenty-three and two over." He then asks the spectator how many matches he has, and the number is, say, sixteen. The performer fulfills his promise and counts out sixteen matches, then seven more to make twenty-three, and has two left in his hands.

If you will analyze the performer's statement, you will see that all he said was that he had twenty-five matches, though he expressed it in such a manner that no one would ever guess this was what he was saying. He might equally well have said, "I have as many matches as you, enough more to make twenty-one and four over," or any other combination that would total twenty-five. It makes no difference, of course, how many matches the spectator takes as long as he takes fewer than twenty, for the performer always takes more than twenty and thus has enough to make up his mysterious total, which, though expressed to the audience in a complicated manner, is, nevertheless, the exact number of matches that he holds in his hand.

TRICKS WITH HANDKERCHIEFS

THE APPEARING HANDKERCHIEF

THIS sleight, while a complete trick in itself, can be used effectively as a preliminary to other handkerchief tricks. The performer shows his hands empty, pulls up his sleeves to prove that there is nothing concealed in them, and then rubs his hands together and produces a lady's handkerchief.

This is accomplished by rolling up a lady's handkerchief into as small a compass as possible and privately secreting it in the crook of the right elbow, hidden from sight by a fold of the coat sleeve. By holding the arm slightly bent, the handkerchief can be easily retained in place and kept out of sight. After showing both hands empty, the performer pulls up his coat sleeves, first the left and then the right, and as he does so he removes the handkerchief from its hiding place with his left thumb and conceals it in the palm of his left hand. The two hands are then immediately brought together and waved up and down, the handkerchief being allowed to work slowly out into sight.

THE HANDKERCHIEF FROM THE POCKET

ANOTHER effective way of magically "appearing" a handkerchief is to produce it from an apparently empty trousers pocket. The performer first pulls his pocket out and shows it to be absolutely empty. His hands are likewise shown to contain nothing. Nevertheless, the pocket is no sooner put back in place than the performer reaches in and removes a handkerchief.

It will be found that a comparatively large handkerchief can be comfortably and securely concealed in the upper inner corner of any trousers pocket. If rolled up into a small ball and tucked into this corner, the pocket can be pulled out and will be apparently perfectly empty, yet the handkerchief is there all the time, and the magician can produce it instantly as soon as the pocket is put back in place.

A handkerchief can, of course, be very effectively "disappeared" in this way, also.

THE HANDKERCHIEF FROM THE COAT POCKET

THIS little sleight will be found both useful and amusing, and can be used with good effect as a preliminary to any trick in which a handkerchief is used. The performer searches his pockets for a handkerchief and evidently finds none, for he asks the audience if they will lend him one. As he stands expectantly before them, a handkerchief suddenly rises from his coat pocket. Somewhat surprised, the performer, nevertheless, grasps it and uses it for his next trick.

A piece of black thread is tied to the center of the

handkerchief and, with the aid of a needle, is passed through the coat about eight or ten inches above the pocket in which the handkerchief is placed. The thread is then led over the performer's shoulder and down his back, the length being adjusted to make it reach almost to the bottom of his coat. A button is tied to the end so that it can be easily gotten hold of. To make the handkerchief rise, the thread is pulled by the hand on the side opposite to the pocket, which should also be the side away from the audience.

THE MAGIC APPEARING KNOT

THE magician holds a handkerchief by one corner between his right thumb and fingers. He takes in his left hand the lower corner diagonally opposite the one he is holding, shows it to the audience, and places it in his right hand. With a quick snap, he releases it, still holding the corner he held originally. Nothing out of the ordinary has happened, so he repeats the process a second and third time, when a knot magically appears in the lower corner.

This is, without doubt, one of the best impromptu handkerchief tricks extant, and should be learned by everyone who aspires to mystify his friends. The secret is, as usual, simplicity itself. Before showing the trick, the performer ties a knot in one corner of the handkerchief. This corner is held in the right hand, the knot being hidden behind his fingers. The first two times the handkerchief is shaken out, the lower, or opposite, corner is released. On the third shake, the lower corner is retained in the right hand and the knotted corner is released.

THE FLYING HANDKERCHIEFS

WITH the aid of the simple apparatus here described, a number of astonishing vanishing and reappearing handkerchief tricks can be done without the slightest fear of detection. A piece of paper is rolled into a cone, or cornucopia shape, a handkerchief is placed inside it, and, Presto!—when the cone is unrolled the handkerchief has disappeared. A handkerchief placed in one cone can be made to vanish and reappear in another empty cone, or in a drinking glass. A handkerchief placed in a cone can be made to change color before the cone is unrolled. Doubtless, other effects of a like nature will occur to the magician as he experiments with the paper cones used for the trick.

Ordinary newspaper is the best material to use for the cones. A double sheet is folded over on the creased center line and pasted together with the exception of a little space along the top near one corner, where the paper is left unpasted so as to form a little pocket just large enough to contain a small handkerchief. To the audience, the paper looks like a single sheet.

To vanish a handkerchief, it is simply tucked into

the little pocket after the paper is rolled up. To transfer a handkerchief from one cone to another, a second piece of paper is prepared as described, and a duplicate handkerchief is hidden in the pocket before showing the trick. To make the handkerchief appear in a glass, a duplicate handkerchief is used, which is rolled up and placed in a handy pocket or on the table close to another larger handkerchief. The glass is shown to be empty, and both the large and the duplicate handkerchiefs are picked up together. The duplicate is dropped into the glass under cover of the large handkerchief, which is at once thrown over the glass to conceal it until the other handkerchief has been vanished by the use of one of the paper cones. To make a handkerchief change color, a piece of paper is prepared with two hidden pockets, and the second handkerchief is concealed in one of them prior to the performance.

THE VANISHING KNOT

THE performer ties a knot in the center of a handkerchief and draws his hand down over it several times. The knot still remains, but once more the hand passes over it, and it magically dematerializes.

The handkerchief used should preferably be a silk one that will slip easily, and the knot should be tied quite loosely. Care is taken not to tighten it the first few times the hand is passed over it. On the last pass, the performer catches his thumb in a fold of the knot and pulls it right down the handkerchief and off the end as his hand descends. The effect is quite startling and practically undetectable, as the secret move is entirely covered by the fingers and back of the hand.

THE SPINNING HANDKERCHIEF

THE performer borrows a handkerchief and places it over the blunt end of a pencil. Rapidly moving the hand holding the pencil in a circle, he spins the handkerchief about on top of the pencil, some mysterious power keeping it from flying off into space.

The mysterious power is, to be sure, no more or less than an ordinary pin or needle which has been driven into the end of the pencil. The center of the handkerchief is impaled on its point.

The trick can be made more effective still by borrowing the pencil from some member of the audience, in which case everybody will know that neither it nor the handkerchief is prepared. The pencil should be one with an eraser attached, and the pin, whose head has been cut off, is pushed into the rubber on the way back to the stage. Since this cannot be done rapidly with the bare fingers, a coin should be held ready in the right hand and used as a pusher.

THE KNOT THAT WON'T STAY TIED

A^S A magical flourish this mysterious knot will
be found both useful and puzzling. The performer ties a single knot in a handkerchief and pulls
on the ends as if to tighten it. Instead, the knot
mysteriously disappears.

When the knot is tied, the performer simply slips
his left thumb between the two ends of the handkerchief, as shown in the illustration. His left forefinger
then closes on the same portion of the handkerchief
opposite the thumb, and the hands are pulled apart,

when the knot naturally ceases to be. If done rapidly the slight shifting of the fingers will be absolutely undetectable, and the audience will never suspect that the left hand is not pulling on the extreme end of the handkerchief.

THE BURNED AND RESTORED HANDKERCHIEF

THIS is the neatest method of executing the burned and restored handkerchief trick, for it requires a minimum of sleight of hand and does away altogether with the necessity of substituting a duplicate handkerchief for the original one.

When the performer starts the trick, he has a small piece of material cut from an old handkerchief concealed in his left hand. A handkerchief is borrowed from some member of the audience and is placed on the palm of the left hand, which closes over it. The end is then apparently drawn out between the thumb and forefinger, but, in reality, the concealed material is drawn out. This is set fire to with a match and allowed to burn down close to the performer's hand, when it is snuffed out, the hand is opened, and the original handkerchief is shown to be unharmed. When putting out the burning fragment with his right fingers, the performer draws it out of the left hand and conceals it in his right, disposing of it at the first opportunity.

THE DISSOLVING KNOTS

THREE or more handkerchiefs are tied together end to end by the spectators, the knots being pulled as tight as they please. Placing them behind his back for an instant, the performer produces them separated from one another, the knots having in some miraculous manner disappeared.

After the spectators have knotted the handkerchiefs, the performer himself gives each knot an additional pull, apparently to make them tighter still. In reality, he pulls on only one of the handkerchiefs, holding it above and below the knot, with the body of the handkerchief in one hand and the short end in the other hand. This has the effect of untwisting the handkerchief and pulling it out in a straight line around which the other handkerchief is twisted. When each knot has been treated in this fashion, a slight pull will suffice to separate each handkerchief from the next one.

THE SELF–UNTYING HANDKERCHIEF

THIS is a handkerchief novelty with a very weird effect. A silk handkerchief is tied in a loose knot and held at arm's length. As the magician makes hypnotic passes over it, the lower end slowly starts to move, comes up through the loop, and unties itself.

The secret of the trick lies in the use of a thin silk handkerchief which will slip easily and a length of black thread. A bent pin is attached to one end of the thread, and the other end is tied around one of the performer's vest buttons. The pin is hooked into the performer's coat lapel or vest while the handkerchief is being twisted up ready for tying. It is then caught in the end of the handkerchief held in the right hand, and the handkerchief is loosely knotted. The corner to which the thread is attached is the lower corner of the knot and hangs downward after the knot is tied, the performer holding the opposite corner in his left hand. By slowly extending the left arm and increasing the tension on the thread, the lower corner will be slowly drawn up through the loop, and the knot will be untied.

THE KNOTTED HANDKERCHIEFS

TWO handkerchiefs are borrowed from the audience, and the performer throws them into the air. As they come down, he catches one of them by the corner, and the other one, instead of falling to the ground, is seen to be mysteriously knotted to the one the performer has caught. Once again they are thrown in the air, and both flutter separately to the ground, the knot having disappeared as mysteriously as it appeared in the first instance.

This effect is obtained by the use of a small rubber

band which the performer secretes in his hand and gets over the tips of his thumb and forefinger just before throwing the handkerchiefs in the air. It is then slipped over an end of each handkerchief, and when they return from their aërial flight they look exactly as though they were knotted together. The performer then takes the knotted ends in his hand and removes the rubber band just before throwing them aloft for the second time. As he stoops to pick up the separated handkerchiefs, he drops the elastic on the floor.

THE HANDKERCHIEF FROM A MATCH FLAME

THIS is an exceptionally neat impromptu method of producing a handkerchief out of thin air, or rather from the flame of a burning match.

The performer takes a box of matches from his pocket, withdraws one, and strikes it. As the flame flares up, he reaches toward it and seems to draw a handkerchief right out of it.

The handkerchief used is a small one such as is used by ladies and before commencing the trick it is concealed inside a match box. The drawer is opened halfway, and the handkerchief is tucked in behind it. The box is then put back in the pocket, still half opened. When the box is withdrawn, the performer opens it a little farther, giving the impression of having opened it all the way. A match is taken out, and the box is closed, thus pushing the handkerchief into the palm of the performer's hand. As soon as the match has been struck on the side of the box, the box is dropped onto the table, the hand containing the handkerchief approaches the flame, and the handkerchief is allowed to slip down to the fingertips and reveal itself to the audience.

BALANCING A HANDKERCHIEF

IF ANY feat seems impossible, it is that of balancing a folded handkerchief on one's fingertip, but the amateur magician is able to show that this is simplicity itself if one only knows how.

The handkerchief is folded diagonally, and a pencil or penholder, whichever is nearest at hand, is secretly rolled up inside it. To keep the handkerchief from unfolding during the course of the trick a small rubber band may be placed around it. When this is done, there will be no difficulty in balancing the handkerchief either on the fingertip, the chin, or the nose.

A RAPID HANDKERCHIEF TIE

THIS is more of a flourish than a trick, but there are many occasion upon which it can be used to good effect. The performer takes the two opposite corners of a handkerchief in his hands, folds his arms, and when the arms are instantly unfolded, there is a knot in the center of the handkerchief.

The trick depends for its success upon how the arms are folded. The right hand, holding one end of the handkerchief, should be placed across the body first. The left arm is then placed underneath the right arm, and the left hand reaches down and picks up the opposite corner of the handkerchief. Thus the right hand is underneath the left upper arm, and the left hand is on top of the right arm. Now, by simply drawing the arms apart, a knot is tied in the handkerchief.

STRETCHING A HANDKERCHIEF

THOUGH the means by which this trick is accomplished are extremely simple, the effect is quite startling. It is an excellent impromptu trick.

The magician folds a handkerchief diagonally and grasps its center with his right hand. He then pulls at the ends with his left hand, and, little by little, the handkerchief stretches out until it is twice its original size.

The secret of the trick lies in the fact that the performer secretly doubles over the center of the handkerchief, the doubling being concealed by the right hand. The doubling is done by the left hand just as it places the handkerchief in the right hand, and, if skilfully executed, will be undetectable.

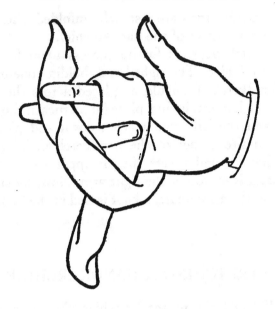

THE INSTANTANEOUS KNOT

THIS is a very pretty handkerchief flourish, which looks easy but which will be found to baffle anyone who tries to do it without being in the secret. The magician places a loosely folded handkerchief over his right hand, waves his hand in the air, and a knot is tied in the center of the handkerchief.

To accomplish this, an ordinary handkerchief is rolled up diagonally and hung over the right hand across the crotch of the thumb. The end hanging down behind the hand should be longer than the end crossing the palm of the hand. To tie the knot, the

hand is projected quickly away from the body, causing the longer end of the handkerchief to be thrown
toward the performer, passing beneath his hand. The
end is caught between the first and second fingers,
as shown in the diagram. The first and second fingers,
still holding this end, are then withdrawn through the
loop of the handkerchief, and the knot is tied.

With a little practice, this sleight can be done
practically instantaneously, and the slight movements of the fingers will be undetectable.

ANOTHER INSTANTANEOUS KNOT

THIS is another effective method of instantly
tying a knot in a handkerchief, in this instance
both hands being employed.

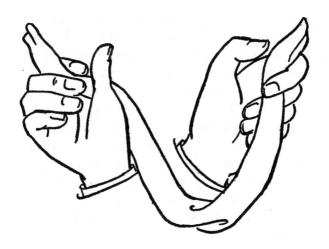

The handkerchief is held as shown in the diagram, with the ends projecting about two inches beyond the fingers. The two hands are then brought quickly together, the thumb and second fingers of the right hand grasp the projecting corner of the handkerchief held in the left hand, and at the same instant the thumb and second fingers of the left hand grasp the corner of the handkerchief held in the right hand. When the hands are separated, a knot is tied in the center of the handkerchief. Since the effect of this sleight depends largely upon the speed with which it is done, it should be carefully practised a number of times before being shown to an audience.

THE GYPSY KNOT

MANY of the gypsy fortune tellers will offer to tell you whether or not your wishes will be granted by the use of a handkerchief whose ends are securely knotted together, the knot being pulled tight by the spectator himself, and then covered over by the folds of the handkerchief. The person who crosses the gypsy's palm with silver holds firmly onto the knot until the word is given to let go, when the gypsy shakes out the handkerchief, and the knot is found to have mysteriously disappeared, signifying, naturally, that the wish has been granted.

To tie such a dissolving knot is very simple, but the effect of the trick is mystifying in the extreme, especially as the spectator has himself tied part of the knot and then pulled it as tight as possible. The secret lies in the way in which the first part of the knot is tied and this is done by the performer. The right end is crossed over the left end on the side toward the performer's body, as shown in the diagram, but then,

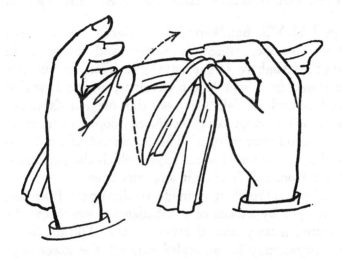

instead of twisting the right end away from him, as would be the case if he were commencing to tie a regular square knot, he twists it toward him and around and under the left portion of the handkerchief as shown by the dotted line in the diagram. There is really no knot at all. The ends are then offered to the spectator, and he is invited to complete the knot, the performer still retaining his hold on the part of the knot already tied. No matter how hard the spectator pulls on his part of the knot, it will be nothing but a twist in the handkerchief and will readily come apart when the handkerchief is given a slight shake.

THE HANDKERCHIEF AND APPLE TRICK

A LADY'S handkerchief is placed in a small envelope, which is sealed and inserted in another slightly larger envelope. This, in turn, is enclosed in a still larger envelope, which is sealed and placed in full view on the magician's table. Presto! The magician gives the envelope to a member of the audience to open. The handkerchief has flown and is rediscovered in an apple, which the performer takes from a dish of fruit and cuts open.

The handkerchief is made to disappear from the envelopes by means of a substitution which can be effected in any one of several ways. The duplicate envelopes may be concealed beneath the lower edge of the performer's vest and changed for the ones containing the handkerchief on the way back to the table, one envelope being tucked under the vest and the other removed with the same motion. Or, if the performer's table is elevated slightly above the audience, the duplicate envelopes may be placed on the table, lying flat, before the performance. In this instance, only the two inner envelopes are prepared in duplicate, the outer one being unnecessary, as will be seen. When the performer returns to his table with the original envelopes, he places them on top of the duplicates, picks both up and rests them against a box or book in full view of the audience. Proceeding with the trick, he picks up both sets of envelopes and tears open the outside one of the three containing the handkerchief. Then, to avoid suspicion, he hands the two inner envelopes to one of the spectators, requesting him to open them. In reality, he hands him the two duplicate envelopes and crumples up the two containing the handkerchief in the outside envelope which he has just torn open.

The handkerchief in the apple is, of course, a duplicate, which was concealed prior to the performance. A small portion of the apple is carefully cut out so as to form a plug, the inside is hollowed out enough to admit the handkerchief, and the plug is replaced, giving the apple a perfectly natural and innocent appearance.

TRICKS WITH CIGARS AND CIGARETTES

AN IMPROMPTU CIGARETTE VANISHER

THE performer rolls up his sleeves, takes the cigarette he is smoking, and pushes it into his closed fist. Upon opening his hand, the cigarette has disappeared.

You can buy the little apparatus needed to do this trick from a magic dealer, but it is so easily and quickly made from a fountain-pen cap and a couple of rubber bands that there is no need to go to the expense of purchasing it. Link two or three rubber bands together, attach one end to a fountain-pen cap by means of the clip, and the other end to a belt loop. The vanisher thus hangs from the belt loop beneath the performer's coat until it is needed.

In vanishing a cigarette, get the vanisher in the right hand and hold it with the open end upright. Turn the right side toward the audience and with the left hand push the cigarette into the closed right hand, really pushing it into the fountain-pen cap. When it is safely inside, open the right hand and the vanisher will fly from sight under the coat, taking the cigarette with it, and the hands are shown to be empty.

THE TURN-AROUND CIGARETTE

THE performer takes a cork-tipped cigarette from a box and pushes it through his closed fist, the tipped end being on the bottom and inserted into the hand first. When the cigarette appears below the hand, it is seen that it has turned over and the tipped end is uppermost.

A plain cigarette is prepared by cutting the cork tip from another cigarette, enlarging it slightly by gluing a small piece of paper between its ends, and fitting it over the end of the first cigarette. The tip should fit loosely enough to slide freely back and forth. When the performer pushes the cigarette through his fist, he grips the movable tip between his fingers and allows the cigarette to slip through it. The tip thus reaches the opposite end of the cigarette during its transit through the hand, and to the audience it appears as though the cigarette had turned upside down.

THE MESMERIZED CIGAR

THE magician borrows a cigar from some member of the audience, or produces one of his own, and, placing it across the fingertips of his right hand, proceeds to make mystic passes with his left hand, explaining, as he does so, that he is mesmerizing it.

When the passes are completed, he slowly tips his right hand, and the cigar adheres to it. The right hand is turned still farther, until the palm is downward, and the cigar still remains in position.

The secret lies in the use of a pin which is held between the second and third fingers of the right hand with the point projecting toward the palm. When the cigar is placed on the fingertips it is pressed against the pin point, which enters it and holds it in place against the fingers, no matter what position the hand assumes.

The effect of the trick can be considerably heightened by a little by-play. After a few passes, the magician tilts his hand, and the cigar falls to the floor. More mesmeric passes are, apparently, necessary, and the magician makes them, until finally, after two or three unsuccessful attempts, the cigar is sufficiently mesmerized and adheres to his hand.

BALANCING A CIGARETTE

THE performer takes a cigarette and sets it upright upon the fingertips of the right hand. Removing his left hand, he moves his right hand about as though trying to keep the cigarette balanced in an upright position, and despite the difficulty of the feat, he succeeds in juggling it so that it retains its perpendicular position.

This trick, like the last one, depends upon a pin,

which is gripped between the fingers of the right hand
and upon whose point the cigarette is placed. It is a
very pretty effect, particularly if the magician makes
it appear as though he were having great difficulty
in making the cigarette maintain its precarious
balance.

THE MAGNETIZED CIGAR

THIS is another very startling method of magnetizing a cigar, and one which has the virtue of
being very little known. In this case, the cigar is
placed against the extended forefinger, to which it
adheres in an upright position.

As before, a pin is used, which is stuck into the
cigar at an acute angle. By resting the projecting part
of the pin on the end of the finger, the cigar will
miraculously remain suspended.

THE GRAVITY DEFYING CIGARETTE

THE performer takes a cigarette from his case and
places it on a table, allowing a good two thirds
of its length to project beyond the table's edge. According to all the laws of gravitation, the cigarette
should fall to the ground, but it, nevertheless, remains where it was placed, owing, no doubt, to the
power of the magician to induce magnetism into
inanimate objects.

The trick is accomplished by slightly moistening the end of the cigarette that is placed on the table. This will make it just adhesive enough to adhere firmly to the table.

LEVITATING A CIGARETTE

IN THIS trick the performer holds a pack of cigarettes in one hand, and, at his word of command, a cigarette leaves the pack and rises to his other hand, which is held above it.

There are several ways of accomplishing this. The simplest, and by no means the least effective, is to remove a cigarette unobserved and place it in back of the pack. The pack is then held with the fingers in front and the thumb in back, and the thumb pushes the cigarette upward.

Another method is to use a black thread, one end of which is attached to a vest button and the other end led through a ring on the second or third finger of the right hand. A piece of wax is attached to this end, which is pressed against one of the cigarettes. By raising the right hand, the tension on the thread is increased and the cigarette is lifted from the pack.

The trick can be made a very effective stage presentation by the use of a third method. In this instance, a number of cigarettes are prepared by attaching small hooks of the hook-and-eye type to them near their upper ends, using either wax or glue.

The back of the case is cut away slightly so that the hooks will not be covered when the cigarettes are inside it.

A length of black thread is then stretched across the stage at about the height of the performer's chin. One end is made fast, and the other end is passed over a hook or through a screw eye located off stage. To this end is attached a weight slightly heavier than a cigarette.

In doing the trick, the performer advances, holding the pack in his left hand. With his right he unobtrusively engages the thread, brings it down, and catches it in one of the hooked cigarettes. As soon as he relaxes the pressure of his left fingers on the pack, the weight will pull the cigarette into the air. This method is particularly effective, as both hands are held absolutely motionless during the entire course of the levitation.

TRICKS WITH NUMBERS

THE MYSTIC ADDITION

THIS is an exceedingly puzzling trick, of which the secret can never be discovered, and which is also very little known.

The performer asks the audience to write down two rows of figures, each row containing five figures. The performer then puts down a third row of figures, the audience a fourth, and the performer a fifth. While the audience is adding up the total, or even before all the figures have been written down, the performer writes a figure on a piece of paper, folds it, and gives it to a member of the audience to hold. When the total is obtained, the performer's paper is opened and the correct total is found upon it.

When the performer writes the third and fifth rows of figures, he puts down figures which will total 9 when added to the figure just above. Thus, if the second row were 12345, the performer would write 87654 for the third line, the 1 and 8, 2 and 7, 3 and 6, 4 and 5, 5 and 4 all totaling 9.

If this is done, the total can always be determined by subtracting 2 from the right-hand figure of the first line and placing 2 before the first figure of the first line. The performer should see to it that the right-hand figure of the first line is not a 1 or 0, since

2 cannot be subtracted from either of these figures without borrowing.

Example:

23697	Audience
41652	Audience
58347	Performer
96531	Audience
03468	Performer

223695

THE CANCELED FIGURE

ONE of the audience is requested to write down a row of figures, as many as he chooses, and then to add them together. When this has been done, the performer asks him to subtract the sum obtained from the original number and then to cancel out any figure he pleases from the remainder. The figures remaining are then added together, and their sum is told to the performer, who at once announces which figure was canceled.

To determine the canceled figure the performer simply subtracts the total given him from the next higher multiple of 9. If the total is a multiple of 9, then no subtraction is necessary, for 9 was the figure canceled.

Suppose the original number to be 32645. These figures added together make 20, which is subtracted from the original number leaving 32625. The spectator then cancels 6, let us say, and adds the remaining figures 3225 which total 12, and tells the performer this figure. The multiple of 9 next higher than 12 is 18, so the performer subtracts 12 from 18 and obtains 6, which is the canceled figure.

MENTAL ARITHMETIC

TO DISCOVER what number a person is thinking of, ask him to subtract 1 from it, multipy the remainder by 2, and add the number first thought of to the product. When the performer is told the total, he adds 3 to it and divides the sum by 3, which gives him the number thought of.

Thus, if 18 was the number thought of, subtracting 1 leaves 17, multiplying this by 2 gives 34, and adding the original number to this gives 52. The performer adds 3, which makes 55, and divides by 3, which gives him 18 or the number thought of.

THE ARITHMETICAL WATCH

THE performer asks one of the spectators to set the hands of a watch at any hour he desires, and then to think of some other hour. The problem is to find out what other hour he has thought of.

Suppose the spectator set the watch at 5 o'clock and thought of 8 o'clock. The performer adds 12 to 5, making 17. He then tells the spectator to subtract the hour at which the hands have been set, namely 5, from 17, and to count the remaining figure, which is 12, on the dial of the watch, starting with the hour just before the one he has thought of, which in this case would be 7, and counting backward. Of course, he will always count 12, and this will invariably cause him to stop counting on the number of which he thought; yet, despite the simplicity of the trick, it will puzzle even the most mathematically minded people.

THE MAGIC TOTAL

THE performer asks one of the audience to write a five-figure number on a piece of paper. Without looking at the number, the performer himself writes something on a piece of paper, folds it, and gives it to a spectator to hold. He then asks the first spectator to reverse his original number and subtract the smaller of the two numbers from the larger. The number thus obtained is then reversed and added to the remainder obtained by the subtraction. When the performer's paper is unfolded, it is found to contain the total last obtained.

Suppose the spectator wrote the number 84312. He reverses this, making 21348, and subtracts the smaller from the larger figure, thus:

$$\begin{array}{r} 84312 \\ -21348 \\ \hline 62964 \end{array}$$

He then reverses the remainder, 62964, making 46926, and adds it thus:

$$\begin{array}{r} 62964 \\ \underline{46926} \\ 109890 \end{array}$$

In practically every instance, the total will be 109890, no matter what number is used, and the performer writes this number on his paper. Every now and then the total will come out 99099, and if the first total (109890) is wrong, the performer simply writes 99099 on another piece of paper and hands it to the audience, allowing them to draw their own conclusions

THE BIRTHDAY NUMBERS

IT IS sometimes next to impossible to get people to tell their age, but by using this necromantic method anybody's age can be obtained without their even knowing it.

Ask the person to think of the number of the month in which his birthday falls, counting January as 1, February as 2, and so on. He must now multiply this number by 2, add 5, multiply the product by 50, and then add his age. From the total subtract 365 and add 115. The last two numbers of this final number will be the person's age, and the first number or numbers will reveal the month in which he was born. If the total is 824, for example, the person would be 24 years old and would have been born in August.

THE SQUARE OF FIFTEENS

THE problem is to place the figures from 1 to 9 inclusive in three rows of three figures each so that they will add up to 15 in eight different directions. This is accomplished as shown in the accompanying cut.

4	9	2
3	5	7
8	1	6

TELLING THE NUMBER THOUGHT OF

THIS is another arithmetical method of quickly finding out what number a person has thought of. Ask him to double his number, multiply the sum by 5, and tell you the product. The number thought of will be the product with the right-hand figure, which will always be a 0 or a 5, cut off.

Thus, if the person thought of the number 11, doubling it would make 22, and multiplying this by 5 would make 110. Cut off the 0 and the original number 11 is left.

THE DEVIL'S WATCH DIAL

THIS little trick will always mystify and will be found to be a very useful addition to the magician's repertoire of impromptu stunts. One of the audience is requested to think of one of the numbers on a watch dial. The performer then taps the dial with a pencil and asks the spectator to add 1 to his chosen number for each tap. When he has counted to 20 in this way, the performer's pencil will be resting on the number thought of.

The performer accomplishes this feat of divination by tapping seven times at random, but on the eighth tap striking 12, on the ninth 11, at the tenth 10, and so on, until the person says that he has reached 20 in his counting, when the pencil will always rest on the chosen number.

WHICH HAND?

THE performer gives a number of pennies to one of the spectators and asks him to place an even number in one hand and an odd number in the other hand. By a simple calculation, he then proceeds to tell him which hand contains the even and which the odd number of pennies.

Ask the spectator to multiply the number in his right hand by an odd figure and the number in his left hand by an even figure, and then tell you if the products added together are odd or even. If the result is an even number, the even number of pennies is in the right hand; if it is odd, the even number is in the left hand.

TRICKS WITH COINS

A SIMPLE COIN VANISH

THIS is one of the simplest coin vanishes to execute and can be used in connection with many tricks in which a coin is disappeared and later made to reappear in some unexpected place.

A dab of wax is affixed to the nail of the middle finger of the right hand, and the coin that is to vanish is put in the palm of the hand near the base of the thumb. A few experiments will show just the right spot in which to place it. To make the coin vanish, the hand is closed and the wax is pressed against the coin, causing it to adhere to the finger nail. The performer then makes a throwing motion and opens his hand, which is seen to be empty.

THE DISAPPEARING COIN

THIS is a very surprising and simple way in which to vanish a coin or to change one coin into another of a different value. The coin to be vanished is placed on the tips of the fingers of the left hand. The fingers of the right hand then approach it and appear to rub it, though in reality they do not actually touch it. This position of the hands brings the left fingertips very close to the right coat sleeve, and, with a sudden motion of the left hand, the coin can be instantaneously shot up the sleeve. The movement is very well covered by the circular motion of the right hand and is practically undetectable, especially if the left hand is kept moving slightly during the rubbing process.

It is very easy to change a dime into a quarter by the use of this same sleight. The quarter is gripped between the first and second fingers of the right hand and is dropped onto the fingertips of the left hand as soon as the dime has been safely shot out of sight.

THE COIN PASS

IT IS frequently necessary for the magician to pretend to transfer a coin or other small object from one hand to the other, in reality retaining it in the original hand, and the pass here described is the most effective way of accomplishing this object.

Hold the coin between the thumb and first and second fingers of the right hand, the palm of the hand being upward. Now bring the left hand toward the right, passing the left thumb under and the fingers over the coin, bringing fingers and thumb together just as they pass the coin. To the audience it will look as though you had grasped the coin, but actually you allow the coin to drop into the palm of the right hand just at the moment when it is hidden from sight by the left hand. The left hand is firmly closed as if it were really holding the coin, and the performer should keep his gaze concentrated upon it, thus attracting the audience's attention to it while his right hand drops naturally to his side.

MULTIPLYING MONEY

A DIME is borrowed from the audience, and the magician states that he is going to demonstrate with it how money makes money. He rubs the dime back and forth along the edge of a table a few times, when it suddenly doubles, and the performer has two coins in his hand. The rubbing process is repeated a second and third time, and each time the coin multiplies itself into two.

The extra dimes are attached with wax or soap to the under side of the table near the edge. The performer rubs the first coin with the ball of his thumb, and in this position his fingers are naturally beneath the edge of the table where they can readily detach the coins affixed there without being detected.

THE HANDKERCHIEF COIN VANISH

THIS is one of the best and simplest means by which a coin can be vanished without the use of sleight of hand. A handkerchief is prepared by sewing a coin in one corner and sewing over it a piece of material similar to that of which the handkerchief is made.

The coin to be vanished is placed in the center of the prepared handkerchief and apparently wrapped up, but in reality the sewed-in coin is enfolded, and the real coin is allowed to slip out into the performer's hand, to be reproduced later in any manner he pleases.

ODD OR EVEN

THE effectiveness of this trick, like that of many others, lies in its simplicity. No matter how many times it is shown, it will repeatedly puzzle an audience.

One of the spectators is given a number of coins and is asked to count them to see if there is an odd or an even number. At the same time the performer takes some coins and states that, when his are added to those held by the spectator, the total will be odd if the spectator holds an even number, and even if the spectator holds an odd number. In effect, whatever number, odd or even, the spectator is holding, the performer will add enough to make just the opposite.

This is accomplished by always adding an odd number of coins to those held by the spectator; for, if you add an odd number to an even number, the result will always be odd, and if an odd number is added to an odd number the total will always be even.

HEADS OR TAILS

A COIN is spun on a table, and the performer, without looking at it, tells whether it falls heads or tails with unvarying success.

The coin used must be prepared beforehand by cutting a little notch on one side of the edge, so that a tiny piece of metal projects from one side of the coin. When the coin is spun, it will spin itself out in the ordinary way if it falls with the notched side uppermost. If, however, it falls with the notched side downwards, it will spin itself out in a much shorter time and finally drop quite suddenly on the table, this being caused by the friction set up by the notch. The difference in sound is too slight to be detected by the audience, but after one or two experiments, the performer can tell at once which way the coin falls.

COINS AND CARDS

THE performer places a dime on the table and asks the audience to draw two cards from the deck. One of the cards is placed over the dime, and the other card is placed beside it. When the cards are lifted, the dime is found to have changed place, and the performer makes it pass back and forth at will, causing it to appear under whichever card the audience selects.

Two dimes are used, and both are prepared by dabbing a bit of wax or soap to one side. One is thrown on the table with the waxed side uppermost, and the other is retained in the performer's hand. When the cards have been drawn, the performer secretly presses the dime in his hand against one of them, causing it to adhere to the face of the card. Thus, when the cards are placed on the table, there is a dime under each of them. When picking up the cards the dimes can either be lifted or left on the table, either by pressing down on the card or bending it slightly lengthwise.

THE RING AND COIN VANISH

A BORROWED coin is placed on a sheet of paper, a small metal ring is placed over it, and a piece of cardboard is put on top of the ring. In a moment the cardboard is removed and the coin has disappeared.

This is quite an old trick, but it is given here, as it forms an excellent prelude to the following trick, which is a new and little-known version.

Any small metal ring about an inch and a half or two inches in diameter, such as a key ring, will do for the trick. A circular piece of paper the same size as the ring is glued to its under side prior to the performance. In executing the trick, the coin is placed on a piece of paper identical with the paper glued to the ring, and when the ring is placed over the coin the paper hides it from sight, though the audience believe that they can see right through the ring to the paper underneath. As soon as the ring is lifted, the coin reappears.

THE NEW RING AND COIN VANISH

THE effect of this trick is identical with that of the one last described, but in the new method the ring is unprepared in any way, and if anyone in the audience asks to examine it expecting to find paper glued to one side, he will be very much surprised to find that it is normal in every way and absolutely without preparation.

The secret of the new method lies in the piece of cardboard that is used to place over the ring. A little square of wood is pasted to the center of the under side of the cardboard, and before showing the trick, a dab of soap or a drop of glue is put on the wood. Thus, when the ring is put over the coin and the cardboard is placed over the ring, the soap or glue adheres to the coin and brings it away when the cardboard is lifted.

VANISHING A SPINNING COIN

THIS is a trick that requires some dexterity to execute properly, but it is extremely deceptive, and is well worth practising a few times in order to gain perfection.

The magician spins a coin, and while it is still spinning claps his right hand over it. At the same time the left hand is placed on the table. The right hand is then lifted, and the coin has vanished, only to be discovered a moment later under the left hand.

When the magician covers the coin with his right hand, he hits it quickly sideways and toward his waiting left hand, which immediately closes over it. The sleight is done so suddenly and is so much a part of the downward motion of the right hand that it takes an exceptionally keen eye to detect it.

AN EFFECTIVE COIN VANISH

THIS is one of the best ways to vanish a coin when you are suddenly called upon to do some impromptu coin tricks.

The coin to be vanished is held between the thumb and fingers of the right hand. The palm of the left hand is then held upward and the coin is placed upon it. The right hand is withdrawn and shown empty, and the left hand is closed over the coin. The performer then extends his left arm upward to its full length, the hand being kept closed. But just before the arm is extended, the coin is allowed to slip out of the hand on the side toward the little finger and into the right hand, which is held in readiness. The right hand should be held naturally against the waist with the fingers partly open, and then, if the left hand is dropped down toward it just before the arm is extended, the transfer can be made very naturally and quickly, the two hands practically touching each other for an instant.

To get rid of the coin, the right hand starts to pull up the left coat sleeve, and the coin is dropped into the breast pocket of the coat.

THE MULTIPLYING HALF DOLLAR

THIS is a new method of instantaneously doubling your money and will be found very effective despite the simple means by which it is accomplished. The trick consists of the performer holding a half dollar between his thumb and fingers and showing all sides of it freely to the audience, turning his hand about to do so. It certainly looks as though there were only a single half dollar, yet a second one suddenly appears at the performer's fingertips.

The second half dollar is concealed behind the first one and is gripped between the thumb and finger in a *horizontal* position. Thus it is completely hidden from the audience by the first half dollar, held vertically in front of it, and by the hand in back of it.

THE COIN IN THE PAPER

A PIECE of plain writing paper is passed for examination, and when it is returned the performer places a borrowed half dollar in its center and folds the paper over so as effectually to enclose the coin. The audience may feel the coin inside the paper, yet it suddenly and mysteriously vanishes.

The explanation is to be found in the manner in which the performer folds the paper. After the first three sides have been folded over, and just before folding the fourth side, the performer tips the paper toward the fourth side, allowing the coin to slip out to the edge of the paper. Thus, when the fourth side is folded, the coin is no longer in the center of the paper, but in the pocket formed by the fourth side, from which it can readily be slipped out into the palm of the hand.

COIN TELEPATHY

THE performer gives a member of the audience two coins of different values, requesting him to grip them in his hands and rest his hands on his knees. The performer then turns his back or leaves the room, but before doing so requests the spectator to think very hard of one of the coins and hold the hand containing it up in front of his eyes while he counts twenty. It is explained that this length of time is necessary to allow the performer to concentrate sufficiently to detect which coin is being thought of. Upon his return to the room, the performer immediately tells which coin was being thought of.

He does so by noting the color of the spectator's hands. When they are rested on his knees, the blood flows down into them, giving them a slightly darker color than usual. Then, when the spectator holds the hand containing the chosen coin in front of his eyes, the blood recedes and leaves this hand distinctly lighter in color than the other.

THE TWENTY-PENNY TRICK

THIS is one of the most ingenious of all impromptu coin tricks, and will never fail to mystify an audience.

The performer borrows twenty pennies from the audience and places them on a plate. While the pennies are being collected, he secretly conceals five other pennies in his left hand. When he gains possession of the plate, he pours the twenty pennies that it holds into his left hand, mixing them with the five already there. These pennies are given to some member of the audience to hold, and the performer asks him to return five of them, leaving, as the spectator supposes, only fifteen pennies in his possession, although he really has twenty.

In the meanwhile, the performer has taken another penny from his pocket and concealed it in his right hand. When the five pennies are returned, he takes them in his left hand and immediately transfers them to his right hand. He then gives the six pennies to another person to hold and asks him to return one of them, reminding him that he now has four pennies and the other spectator fifteen.

The performer then takes the single penny that has just been returned to him and, by means of the pass already described, pretends to transfer it to his left hand, in reality retaining it in his right hand and dropping it on the table or into his pocket at the first opportunity. Now he commands the penny to fly into the hands of the person who is supposedly holding four pennies. Opening his left hand, the performer shows it to be empty, and, upon the spectator opening his hand, he finds that the penny has flown into it and he has five instead of four. The performer then takes the five pennies that were returned to him by the first spectator and by the same means appears to pass them back into his hands, which, upon being opened, are found to contain the original twenty pennies.

THE FLYING COINS

THIS is a very simple little coin transference, but it is as impressive in effect as many other more elaborate coin changes.

A penny is wrapped up in a handkerchief and given to a member of the audience to hold. A five-cent piece is then wrapped up in a second handkerchief and given to another member of the audience. The magician then commands the coins to change places, and, when the handkerchiefs are unfolded, this is found to have taken place.

The secret lies in the use of two five-cent pieces,

one of which the performer secretes in his right hand before commencing the trick, gripping it in the crook of his thumb. The other five-cent piece and the penny are placed on the table in full view. Picking up the penny, the performer places it in the center of the first handkerchief and pretends to wrap it up, but before folding over the handkerchief, he drops the concealed five-cent piece into it and removes the penny, tucking it into the place previously occupied by the five-cent piece.

The other five-cent piece is then picked up and apparently wrapped in the second handkerchief, but the penny is substituted for it in the same manner as the previous change was effected. On unfolding the handkerchiefs, the coins will have mysteriously changed places.

THE OBEDIENT COIN

THIS is a handy trick for the amateur magician's repertoire, as people frequently ask to be shown a trick at the dinner table and this one requires a table with a cloth upon it.

The magician places two half dollars on the table, lays a dime between them, and then rests a glass on the two half dollars. The trick is to remove the dime without touching either the glass or the half dollars.

The dime can easily be moved out from under its impromptu prison by scratching the tablecloth near it with the nail of the forefinger.

AN IMPROMPTU COIN VANISHER

A VERY effective impromptu apparatus for vanishing a coin can be made from a penny match box at a moment's notice. Take an ordinary safety match box, and while you are removing the matches run your finger nail along one end of the bottom of the drawer, separating the bottom from the upright end piece. Then loosen the sides of the end piece for about a quarter of an inch from the bottom, which can also be done very simply and quickly by an effective use of your finger nails. In this way, a little hinged flap is formed, running from side to side of the bottom of the end piece of the drawer.

Any coin that is now placed inside the box can be made to disappear by simply allowing it to slide out into your hand through the small opening in the end of the drawer. The flap is then pressed back into place, and the box looks as though it had never been tampered with.

WHERE DID IT GO?

THIS is a new and very surprising method of disappearing a coin.

The performer takes a penny or a ten-cent piece and spins it on the table. While it is still spinning, he places a match box on top of it and asks the audience to guess whether it fell heads or tails. When they have guessed, he lifts the match box, and the coin is found to have disappeared.

Before doing the trick, empty a penny match box, and while doing so split the bottom unobserved with your finger nail in order to weaken it. When you place the match box on top of the spinning coin, you do so rapidly and with enough force to push the coin right through the bottom of the box.

The coin can then be reproduced from the inside of the box or vanished from it by the method just described, only to reappear in a subsequent trick.

THE TUBE AND COIN DISAPPEARANCE

THE magician exhibits a paper tube which he proves to be hollow and empty by dropping a pencil through it. The tube is then set upright on a plate, and a coin is dropped into it. Everyone hears the coin strike the plate, yet, when the tube is lifted, the coin has disappeared.

The secret lies in the construction of the tube. A piece of paper is rolled up and secured in tube shape with a rubber band. In one end there is glued a circular piece of paper with a hole slightly larger than the diameter of a pencil cut in its center. The pencil is dropped through this hole. When the tube is placed on the plate, the prepared end is on the bottom, but the paper is not thick enough to muffle the sound of the coin as it strikes the plate. When the tube is lifted the coin, of course, is brought away with it.

CATCHING A COIN ON A PLATE

THIS trick can be used to very good advantage as a sequel to the one just described. Picking up another plate, which he shows to be empty, the performer waves it through the air and catches the vanished coin upon it.

The coin is a duplicate which is attached to one end of a length of black thread by means of wax. The thread is led through a hole bored in the bottom of the plate and tied to a vest button. The duplicate coin is kept in the right lower vest pocket until it is required, when it is taken in the right hand. The plate is held in the left hand and waved about a few times, when a sudden lunge is made, the right hand releases the coin, and the tension on the thread brings it instantaneously to the center of the plate.

THE MONEY BOX

THE performer exhibits a cardboard candy box, showing both the box and the cover to be empty and unprepared. A coin is placed inside the box, the cover is put on, and the performer shakes the box. The sound emanating from it is greater than would be made by a single coin, and, upon removing the cover, it is found that the original coin has multiplied into ten or a dozen coins.

This is a new and very clever kind of money box, which has many advantages over the forms previously in use. In the present trick the box is prepared by sticking a number of coins to the inside of the cover by means of wax or soft soap. The coins are then covered with a piece of cardboard cut to fit within the cover. It should be cut so that it fits quite snugly inside the cover and yet is loose enough to drop off when the cover is put on the box.

The working of the trick should now be clear. At the commencement, the cover is lying upside down on the table with the cardboard in place over the coins. The box is shown empty, and the cover as well, the performer taking care not to invert it. After placing the single coin in the box, the cover is put on, the cardboard drops to the bottom of the box, and a slight shake dislodges the coins attached to the cover.

MONEY FROM THE AIR

THIS is another experiment in multiplying money showing how the magician can speed up the workings of compound interest so as to far more than double his money in the twinkling of an eye. Borrowing a dollar bill from one of the audience, the performer holds it at his fingertips and shows that both hands are empty except for the single "greenback."

Waving his hand in the air, there are suddenly a dozen or more dollar bills, which have apparently materialized from the atmosphere.

The extra bills are rolled up tightly before showing the trick and secreted in the bend of the left elbow, where they are concealed by a fold of the coat sleeve. After showing his hands empty, the performer pulls up his sleeves, bringing away the bills in his right hand as he does so. It is now an easy matter to unroll them and cause them to appear at the fingertips while the hand is being waved about in the air.

THE COIN IN THE ORANGE

AFTER vanishing a coin by one of the methods already described, the performer allows the audience to select an orange from a plate which contains several. The orange is in no way prepared, yet when it is cut open the vanished coin is found inside it.

The method of introducing the coin into the orange is very ingenious and far superior to the old method, in which a slit had to be previously cut in one of the oranges. The coin is retained in the palm of the performer's left hand, and the selected orange is also placed in his left hand. The orange is cut in two halves and is turned around in the hand as the cutting proceeds. When the part that was first cut is thus revolved until it is toward the back of the hand, the coin is pushed into the cut and to the center of the orange. As soon as this has been done, it is well to hold the orange by the fingers only until the cutting is completed, thus allowing the audience to see that there is no last-minute sleight.

THE MYSTIC COIN

ANY coin can be rapidly changed from a perfectly ordinary piece of currency into a mystic coin which will vanish from the performer's hand and reappear instantly, with sleeves rolled up and the hand held at arm's length from the body. This coin can be used in connection with any trick that requires a disappearance, and will be found extremely useful in many ways.

The coin is prepared by gluing to one of its sides the two ends of a short piece of flesh-colored thread. The loop formed by the thread should be just long enough to fit over the thumb and permit the coin to rest in the center of the palm.

To vanish the coin, it is placed on the palm of either hand with the loop over the thumb. Tossing the hand in the air as if to throw the coin away, it is flipped over to the back of the hand and the palm is shown empty. It can also be vanished by closing the hand upon it and allowing it to slip through the fingers. The hand can then be opened and shown empty, though the fingers, of course, cannot be spread apart.

THE MELTED COIN

THIS trick will be found useful when you are suddenly called upon to "do some magic" and are unprepared for anything elaborate. A coin is borrowed, and the performer, holding it in his left fingertips, rubs it against his right coat sleeve just above the elbow. The right forearm is held vertically. The heat induced by the friction, or so the performer says, gradually melts the metal, and the coin vanishes into thin air.

After rubbing the coin back and forth a few times, it is dropped, as if by accident, on the table or floor. The right hand picks it up and apparently places it in the left, but in reality it is retained in the right hand. The left fingers are immediately placed against the coat sleeve and moved briskly back and forth until the performer is ready to reveal the coin's disappearance. The performer can produce the coin from a spectator's nose or ear, from his pocket, or in any other manner he pleases.

THE PAPER CONE AND COINS

THE magician rolls a piece of newspaper into a cone which he places point downward in a glass. Picking up a coin, he causes it to vanish. He then lifts up the cone and inverts it, and the coin falls out of it onto the table.

The newspaper is prepared by pasting to it, near its center, a small piece cut from another newspaper. This piece should be just large enough to form a pocket in which the coin to be used will fit comfortably. It is pasted around three sides only, the top being left open, and a duplicate coin is tucked into the pocket before the performance. The other coin can be vanished in any of the ways already described.

HANDKERCHIEF, COIN, AND MATCH BOX

A COIN is wrapped up in a handkerchief and given to some member of the audience to hold, and a match box is then emptied of its contents and placed on the table in full view of everybody. Seizing one corner of the handkerchief, the magician jerks it away from the spectator's grasp. The coin has vanished and is found in the match box by one of the spectators, who is asked to look there.

The handkerchief is prepared by sewing a coin in the corner as previously described, and the coin that is shown the audience is retained in the performer's hand when he pretends to wrap it up. When he reaches into his pocket for the match box, he leaves the coin in the pocket.

A duplicate coin is concealed between the inside cover of the match box and one end of the drawer, which is pushed open a little more than halfway. A number of matches are put in the drawer, and the box is put in the pocket with the drawer open as described. The act of shutting the drawer after the matches have been removed dislodges the coin and causes it to fall into the box, where it is later found by the audience.

THE BALANCED COIN

THIS is one of the best impromptu coin effects, and has the advantage of requiring no preparation or sleight of hand. A half dollar is borrowed from one of the audience, and the performer proceeds to balance it on its edge on his outstretched fingers. Waving his hand over it, he motions it to lie down, and the coin slowly falls backward until it is lying flat on the hand. Both hands are immediately shown to be empty except for the coin.

The secret lies in the use of a pin, which is gripped in an upright position between the first and second fingers. The coin is placed in front of the pin and resting against it, so it also stands upright. By gradually relaxing the grip of the fingers, the coin is allowed to fall slowly backward. To finish the trick, throw the coin in the air, at the same time spreading the fingers and allowing the pin to fall to the floor. Catch the coin in the other hand and show both it and your hands to the audience to prove that there has been no deception.

THE CLIMBING COIN

THE simplicity of this trick is, perhaps, its strongest point, and though it may not seem to be a very startling effect, just try it and you will be surprised at the results. A coin is borrowed and dropped into a drinking glass. For a moment it rests on the bottom and then slowly climbs up the side of the glass until it reaches the rim, when the performer takes it in his hand and gives it to the audience to examine before returning it to its owner.

The coin is made to climb with the aid of the magician's most faithful assistant—a piece of black thread. One end of the thread is tied around a vest button, and a piece of wax is attached to the free end. When the coin is received, it is fastened to the thread by means of the wax before being dropped into the glass. Then, by gradually moving the glass away from the body, the coin is made to climb out.

THE SPIRIT COIN

THIS trick, though extremely simple in execution, can be made to create a very profound effect if presented carefully and with a proper atmosphere of mystery. A borrowed coin is dropped into a glass, and the audience is requested to ask questions of the spirits which the magician has summoned to take control of the coin. To answer a question "Yes" the coin jumps up and down twice, making two distinct "tings" against the glass; to answer "No" the coin jumps once. It also raps out numbers and can refuse to answer by jumping angrily up and down a number of times in succession.

A length of black thread with a piece of wax attached to one end is responsible for the manifestations. If possible, the thread should run over a lighting fixture directly over the glass and to an assistant seated with the audience but at one side, where one of his hands will be out of sight. If this is not practicable, the magician can manipulate the thread himself, standing sideways to the audience and using the hand that is on the side away from them.

THE TRAVELING COINS

THIS is a very deceptive trick, which is apparently done by means of a clever substitution, or so the audience is led to believe, but which really requires no sleight of hand at all.

A quarter and a dime are borrowed from the audience. The quarter is put in a match box and a circle is marked on one end of the drawer. The dime is then put in another match box, and a cross is marked on the drawer. The two boxes are placed on the table, the magician pronounces the magic word "Abracadabra," and upon opening the boxes, the coins are found to have changed places, the quarter being in the box marked with a cross and the dime in the box marked with a circle.

Prior to the performance, the magician marks two match boxes, one with a cross and one with a circle. The marks are put on one end of the drawer of each box, and the marked ends are, of course, not shown to the audience. In doing the trick, the quarter is put in the box marked with a cross and a circle is marked on the opposite end of the drawer in full view of the audience. The dime is put in the box previously marked with a circle and the opposite end is marked with a cross. When the performer puts the boxes on the table, he simply turns them around, thus showing the previously made marks.

PASSING A COIN THROUGH A TABLE

THE performer places four coins on the table and then picks one up with his left hand, which he puts under the table. The remaining three coins are covered with the right hand. In a moment he brings up his left hand, which now contains two coins instead of one, and upon lifting his right hand there are only two coins on the table. One of them has, apparently, passed right through the table.

Before showing the trick, an extra coin is fastened to the under side of the table by means of wax. It is brought up in the left hand together with the coin removed from the table. The coins on the table are reduced from three to two by a simple but very clever ruse. At the beginning of the trick, they are placed close to the edge of the table and are later pushed away from the edge by the right hand. In reality, the right hand pushes only two of the coins, allowing one coin to remain behind. This one is covered with the right wrist and is drawn to the edge of the table and dropped into the lap when the right hand is lifted.

THE DISSOLVING COIN

THE magician borrows a half dollar and places it in the center of a handkerchief which is spread out over his left hand. He then grips the coin through the folds of the handkerchief with the thumb and fingers of his left hand and turns his hand over so that the folds of the handkerchief hang downward. With his right hand he makes a few twists in the handkerchief just below the coin so that everybody can clearly see that it is safely wrapped up *inside* the handkerchief.

He then explains that he is able to dematerialize the coin and split it up into its atoms, and that these atoms are so tiny that they will slip through the meshes of the handkerchief. This statement he proceeds to prove by mysteriously drawing the coin right through the fabric of the handkerchief.

This very pretty impromptu trick is done as follows. After the half dollar is placed in the center of the handkerchief, and just before the performer turns his hand over, he slides his left thumb across the face of the coin, thus covering it with a fold of the handkerchief. He now turns his left hand over, but at the same time takes the handkerchief in his right hand, grasping the coin between his thumb and fingers and being careful to keep the fold made by the left thumb in place. The right hand is immediately turned over, and the left hand once again grips the handkerchief, this time enclosing it just below the coin, thus leaving the coin in plain sight above the hand and apparently tightly wrapped in the handkerchief. In reality, the coin is merely in a fold of the handkerchief and should be gradually worked out as though it were being worked right through the fabric.

THE ADHESIVE COIN

THIS is a startling magnetic effect, which is achieved by the use of a prepared coin, and the amateur magician would find it worth his while to carry one of these coins in his pocket all the time, so as to be ready to respond to the request to do some magic, which he is certain to encounter at frequent intervals. In effect, the magician places the edge of a coin against a door, and it mysteriously stays there, defying all the laws of gravity.

The coin is prepared by cutting two small notches close together in its edge. Between the notches there will be a sharp projecting point, which can be pushed into any wooden surface far enough to support the weight of the coin.

THE X-RAY COIN TRICK

A HALF dollar is placed on the table, and while the performer turns his back, the spectators place over it one of three circular cardboard covers. Turning around, the performer apparently sees right through the covers, for he immediately tells which one is over the coin.

The covers consist of three pill boxes, which can be easily obtained. The coin is prepared by fastening a single hair to one of its sides by means of wax or a tiny dab of glue. The hair is so thin that it will be unnoticeable even at close quarters, yet, when the coin is covered, the hair will project beyond the cover, and the performer can always detect it by means of a close scrutiny.

THE PENETRATING COIN

THE performer borrows a coin and drops it down his coat sleeve. Upon rubbing his elbow briskly for a moment or two, he manages to extract the coin right through the cloth, though it is in as sound condition after the trick as before it.

Before showing the trick, the performer pushes a duplicate coin between the buttons on the cuff of his coat sleeve. In this position, it is out of sight and, if wedged tightly into place, it will not fall out. After the first coin has been dropped, the hand moves naturally down toward the elbow, dislodging the duplicate coin as it does so, and producing it after rubbing the elbow a few times to set the audience on the wrong track.

MIXED MULTIPLICATION

THE magician places three coins on the table and picks them up one at a time, counting "One, two, three." Laying them down again, he counts "Four, five, six." Once more he picks them up, counting, "Seven, eight, nine," but as he says "Nine," he picks the coin up and immediately replaces it on the table. He then puts the other two down, counting, "Ten, eleven" as he does so. To all appearances the three coins have been counted four times and the total is eleven instead of twelve.

There will probably be some member of the audience who thinks he sees how the trick is done, and if this is the case, give him the coins and tell him to see if he can do it. He will fail every time, because the coins must be on the table at the commencement of the trick and if you put them in his hands he will start by laying them down instead of picking them up, thus making failure inevitable.

TRICKS WITH DICE AND DOMINOES

THE MAGICIAN'S PAIR O' DICE

THIS is a very impressive little trick and never fails to interest an audience, even though it is understood that it is worked solely on arithmetical principles. In effect, the performer leaves the room, one of the spectators throws two dice on a table, and the performer then tells him what numbers he has thrown.

The arithmetic involved is as follows. As soon as the dice have been thrown, the magician asks the spectator to take the uppermost number on either one of the dice and multiply it by 2, then add 5 to the product and multiply the sum thus obtained by 5. The last step is to add the uppermost number on the other die to this figure, and when the magician is told the total figure, he at once announces the number of spots uppermost on each of the dice.

The magician himself has no complicated figuring to do. His only calculation is to subtract 25 from the last total calculated by the person who has thrown the dice. The remainder that he obtains in this way will be a two-number figure. One of these figures will indicate the number of spots uppermost on one of the dice, and the other figure will indicate the spots showing on the second die. Thus, if the total obtained by the spectator was 60 the performer would subtract 25, obtaining a balance of 35. One of the die would have 3 spots showing and the other dice 5 spots.

NAMING THE UNSEEN DIE SPOTS

WHILE the performer turns his back, three dice are set one on top of the other by the audience. When the performer turns around, he at once tells the total of the spots on the tops and bottoms of the two lower dice and the bottom of the third and uppermost die.

If you will examine a die, you will see that the spots on two opposite sides always total 7. Thus the total of the spots on the tops and bottoms of all three dice would be 21, and to name the total of the hidden spots as enumerated above, all the performer has to do is to subtract the number of spots on the top of the uppermost die from 21.

THE DICE IN THE GLASS

THIS is another clever trick worked on the same principle as the one just described. The performer gives three dice and an ordinary drinking glass to the audience and requests them to drop the dice into the glass. The performer then names the total of the spots on the bottoms of the dice, and when the glass is held aloft, his guess is found to be correct.

Since the total of all three tops and bottoms will always be 21, the performer simply adds the spots showing on the tops of the dice and subtracts this sum from 21, which will give him the total of the spots on the bottoms.

THE MAGNETIC DICE

THE magician takes two dice and places one on top of the other. After a few mystic passes, he takes hold of the top die and lifts it from the table, when it is seen that the bottom die is clinging to it in some mysterious manner. The dice are then separated and shown to be unprepared in any way; nor are there any traces of glue, wax, or any other adhesive substance.

A little moisture applied to the bottom of the upper die is the solution of the mystery. The tip of the right forefinger is moistened with the tongue and then applied to the die. By pressing down firmly when putting the top die in place, it will stick fast to the lower die and bring it along with it when it is lifted.

THE TRANSFERRED DOMINOES

TWENTY or more dominoes are laid face down on the table, and the performer then requests the audience to move any number of dominoes they choose from the end of the line at the performer's right to the opposite end. The only restriction is that they must be moved one at a time. The performer leaves the room while this is being done, and upon his return he immediately turns over a domino whose spots total the number of dominoes moved.

In putting down the dominoes the spots on the domino at the left end of the line should total 12, those of the next 11, of the next 10, and so on, down to the double blank. After the first thirteen dominoes on the left of the line have been arranged in this manner, any number of other dominoes can be added on to the right. Now, if the thirteenth domino from the left is turned up when the performer returns to the room, the total of its spots will invariably equal the number of transferred dominoes.

THE DOMINO MIND READER

WHILE the performer leaves the room, the audience arranges a set of dominoes face downward in a row, starting with any one they wish, but arranging them as though they were playing a game of dominoes, that is, putting a three next to a three, a five next to a five, and so on. When this has been done, the performer, without even entering the room, announces the numbers at each end of the row.

The secret lies in the fact that the performer privately removes one of the dominoes before showing the trick. Whatever numbers are on the domino he has removed will be the end numbers of the audience's row. Suppose he takes a three-four. The end numbers will then be three and four, and so on. The performer should only be careful never to take a double number such as six-six or three-three, for if this is done the trick will not work out.

DICE DIVINATION

ONE of the audience throws three dice on the table and adds together the uppermost spots. The performer, who is blindfolded, then picks up one of them and asks the spectator to add the number of spots on the side nearest him to the total already obtained. Throwing this die on the table, the performer asks the spectator to add the spots on its uppermost side to his previous figure. Removing the blindfold, he looks at the dice as they lie on the table, and at once announces the total figure computed by the spectator.

The secret of this trick lies in the fact that the performer shows the spectator the reverse, or bottom, side of the die that he picks up. If this is done, the spectator's total can always be discovered by adding seven to the total of the uppermost spots of the dice as they last lie on the table when the performer removes his blindfold.

EXPERIMENTS IN MAGNETISM

THE experiments included under this head are tricks that have been, and are being, shown on the professional stage by two classes of performers: professional strong men, and those who claim that they are able to induce powerful electro-magnetism in their own bodies. The latter claim is naturally the more mystifying, as people are ordinarily unaware of the exact properties of electro-magnetism and will believe almost anything that the magician sees fit to tell them. As a matter of fact, all the experiments are based on little-known peculiarities of physical law. If performed as a group, they afford a very interesting and unusual entertainment.

THE HAND AND HEAD TRICK

THIS is one of the simplest "magnetic" tricks, but it is one of the most effective. The performer places one of his hands on top of his head and asks someone in the audience to try to lift it off. The magnetism that runs from the performer's head to his hand is so powerful, however, that no one can succeed in accomplishing this seemingly easy feat.

No strength is needed to keep the hand on the head, for it is practically impossible for anyone to lift it when placed in the position described. A good effect can be obtained by "magnetizing" one of the ladies in the audience and having the gentlemen present try their luck at lifting her hand. She will have no trouble at all in frustrating their greatest efforts.

As a climax to the experiment, the performer can clasp both his hands together on top of his head and have two men on each side of him push upward against his arms. In this way, he will be lifted right off the floor, but his hands will remain "magnetized" to his head.

THE FINGERTIP TRICK

THIS time it is the tips of the performer's two forefingers that are "magnetized." He places them together with his arms held shoulder high, the right forefinger pointing to the left and the left fore-

finger pointing to the right. The hands are brought
in to the body so that they just touch the chest.

Now let someone try to separate the fingertips.
It is an impossibility so long as the person exerts a
steady pull in each direction and does not try to jerk
the hands apart. As soon as the magician cries,
"Presto!" the "magnetism" vanishes (the arms are
relaxed), and the weakest person in the audience can
easily separate the fingers; but, whenever he wishes,
the performer can make them cling together again
like adamant.

THE BROOMSTICK TRICK

A COMMON broomstick is passed for examination, and one of the strongest members of the
audience is asked to hold it horizontally in front of
him with his hands about three feet apart. The performer stands before him on one foot, places the tip
of his right thumb against the broomstick, and tells
the spectator to try to push him over backward. No
matter how hard he tries, it will be found impossible
to make the performer lose his balance.

The secret is simply an application of a physical
law. As the spectator pushes forward, the performer
pushes his thumb upward. It takes only a very slight
pressure to push the broomstick sufficiently out of
the horizontal so that the spectator will require more
strength than he possesses to counteract the upward
movement. Accordingly, all his efforts are expended in

trying to hold the stick down instead of pushing it forward against the performer.

THE HORIZONTAL CHAIR TRICK

ONE of the spectators is asked to hold a chair in such a position that its back passes beneath his left arm and its seat is pressed against his stomach. The hands grip the rungs on the back and front of the chair and hold it horizontally. The performer places his two thumbs against the bottoms of the two uppermost legs and asks the spectator to push him over backward if he can.

It is impossible to do so, since, as in the broomstick trick, the performer pushes upward and thus forces the spectator to dissipate his strength in the effort to bring the chair down to the horizontal.

THE BROOMSTICK AND CIRCLE TRICK

THE performer draws a six-inch circle on the floor, or, if this is not practicable, places a sheet of notepaper on the floor. Three spectators are then requested to grip a broomstick near its upper end, holding it directly over the paper with its lower end about a foot above the ground. The performer then places his hand against one side of the broomstick a few inches from the lower end and tells the spectators

to see if they can push the stick straight down until
it rests on the center of the paper. They are unable
to do so, and, indeed, are lucky if they can hit the
paper at all.

To accomplish his part of the trick, the performer
has merely to push the stick gently to one side with
his hand. So great a leverage is afforded him that a
slight pressure will effectually frustrate the spectator's
efforts.

THE LIFTING TRICK

THIS trick has become quite celebrated owing to
the mystifying manner in which it has been
presented on the professional stage by Annie Abbott,
the famous "Georgia Magnet." Miss Abbott first
allowed two men to lift her off the ground and then
defied the efforts of five men to so much as budge her
heels from the floor. The effect is extremely surprising
and is eminently suitable for parlor or amateur
presentation.

When the performer allows himself to be lifted, he
crooks his arms, so that his hands are pointing upward, and holds his arms close in against the body.
If he does not weigh more than 150 pounds, two men
can now lift him quite easily by the elbows. To make
it impossible for the five men to lift him, the performer assumes the same position, but relaxes all his
arm muscles, allowing them to hang as loosely as
possible from the shoulders. This simple move makes

all the difference in the world and quite adequately frustrates the would-be lifter's greatest exertions.

THE MAGNETIZED CHAIR

A PIECE of newspaper is placed on the floor, and a chair is placed on top of it. Three men from the audience are asked to lift the chair and hold it directly over the paper and about two feet off the ground. Placing the palm of his right hand on one of the side edges of the chair's seat, the performer asks the men to push the chair downward so that all its legs will rest on the paper, a simple request which, nevertheless, they find beyond their powers to accomplish.

As the men push downward, the performer pushes sideways with the heel of his palm and swings the chair out of line. The effort required is so slight that no one will realize that the performer is so much as moving a single muscle.

PARLOR TRICKS

THE tricks included under this head are all of the nature of hoaxes, many of them depending upon a double meaning which is not apparent to the audience. Though they cannot be classed as genuine magic, they are all excellent laugh producers, and the amateur magician will find many ways of working them in, in connection with his more serious efforts at mystifying.

THE LABORS OF HERCULES

NO ONE thinks it very difficult to lift a match or to carry it a few feet, yet the performer tells one of his spectators that he is able to bewitch a match in such a way that he will be absolutely tired out before he has carried it out of the room. When a subject for the experiment has been chosen, the performer takes a knife, cuts off a tiny sliver of the match, and asks him to carry it out of the room. When he returns, the performer gives him another and still another, until the spectator actually grows tired or realizes the impracticability of carrying out his part of the performance, since the performer can keep him running to and fro for hours before all the match has been cut up and carried out.

THE THREE COINS

THE performer places three coins in a row on the table and asks his audience if they are able to remove the middle coin from its position without touching it. When all admit that they do not see how this can be done, the performer calmly picks up the right-hand coin and places it on the left end of the row. The middle coin is now no longer in the middle and has therefore been removed from its position without being touched.

PARLOR THOUGHT TRANSFERENCE

THE audience is furnished with a piece of paper and several members are requested to write a single word upon it. No matter what is written, the performer announces his intention of writing the same words on another piece of paper. While the audience is writing, the performer sits plunged in meditation, but as soon as they have finished he writes on his paper and announces that he is ready for the test. "Will somebody please read what has been written? I believe I have written the same words on my piece of paper." As soon as the audience's words have been read, the performer exhibits his paper on which he has written "the same words," thereby fulfilling his promise.

THE MAGIC CIRCLE

THE magician places one of the spectators in the center of the room and makes a number of mysterious hypnotic passes over him. He then takes a piece of chalk, or a pencil, and tells him that he will draw a circle around him which he will not be able to walk out of, even though his legs are not bound or fastened in any way. When everyone is thoroughly mystified and prepared to witness a real demonstration of hypnotism, the performer draws the magic circle around the waist of the spectator's coat.

WALKING THROUGH A VISITING CARD

THE performer takes a visiting card, or a piece of paper of the same size, and proposes to cut a hole in it through which he will be able to walk. This apparently absurd statement is no more than the simple truth, for if the card is cut as shown in the accompanying diagram, it can be drawn out to form a surprisingly large loop through which the performer will have no difficulty in walking, if he stoops over a trifle.

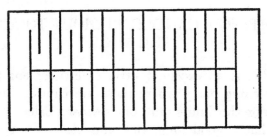

THE VISIBLE INVISIBLE

IF YOU are called upon for an after-dinner trick, this will be sure to amuse your audience and mystify them as well, until you show them how it is done. Picking up a napkin ring, or other small object from the table, the magician tells the person seated next him that he will put it in a place where every person in the room, with the exception of himself, will be able to see it. No blindfold will be used, nor will the magician restrain him from turning around or moving about the room in search of the vanished object. It is simply a case of the magician having a hypnotic will, which can cause the subject of the experiment to be temporarily blind in so far as the napkin ring is concerned.

The trick is accomplished by placing the napkin ring on top of the person's head, but the performer should be careful to see that there are no mirrors in the room.

LIGHTING A CANDLE WITHOUT TOUCHING THE WICK

THIS is an excellent little divertissement for an evening party where there are candles burning, either on the dining table or elsewhere. Select a candle that has a good long wick and blow it out with a sudden breath. Now, if a lighted match is held two or three inches above the wick, the flame will travel down the smoke and relight the candle.

The performer should preface the trick by telling what he is going to do: namely, light the candle without touching the match to the wick which, of course, sounds like an impossibility.

THE RING AND PENCIL TRICK

A FINGER ring is borrowed and placed over a pencil, one of the spectators being requested to hold both ends of the pencil to keep the ring from slipping off. The performer then proposes to take the ring off the pencil without removing the spectator's hands.

A moment's reflection will show that this can be very easily done by simply lifting the ring up and holding it so it does not touch the pencil, even though the pencil is still running through its center.

INVISIBLE BARRIERS

THIS is an excellent drawing-room trick and one which never fails to get a good laugh. The performer spreads a newspaper out on the floor and asks two people to stand on it. He then proposes to use his magic powers so as to make it impossible for them to touch each other, even though they are both standing on the small area of the paper. When the audience express their disbelief in his ability to accomplish this seemingly impossible feat, he proceeds to show them that it can be done by simply placing the newspaper in a doorway. Now the people can stand upon it, and yet, when the door is closed, it will be impossible for them to touch each other.

THE BEWITCHED GLASS

THE performer offers to fill a glass with water in such a way that no one in the audience will be able to lift it from the table without spilling every drop it contains. When the glass has been filled, the performer places a piece of heavy paper over the top, turns the glass quickly upside down, and then draws away the paper, leaving the glass standing upside down on the table. Now it will, of course, be impossible for anyone to lift it from the table without spilling the entire contents.

TRICKS WITH PAPER

THE CIGARETTE–PAPER TRICK

THE famous torn and restored cigarette-paper trick should be included in the repertoire of every magician for, though simple of execution, it is one of the most mystifying impromptu tricks in existence and has fooled thousands. In effect, the performer tears a cigarette paper into pieces and rolls them together into a tiny ball. The ball is immediately unrolled, and the paper is found to be in its original condition.

A duplicate piece of paper is used which, prior to the performance, has been rolled into a ball and secreted between the first and second fingers of the left hand. It is held near the tips of the fingers and on the inner side of the hand. It is so small that the hand and fingers can be held perfectly naturally all the time. The original paper is torn up and rolled into a ball and apparently transferred from the right to the left hand. In reality it is retained in the right hand, being gripped between the first and second fingers, and the duplicate ball is pushed to the left fingertips.

If the magician is working at some distance from his audience, the original paper may be dropped on the floor; but if he is working at close quarters, the best method is to put his right fingers to his mouth, ostensibly to moisten them, and to leave the original paper in his mouth.

THE NAPKIN-TEARING TRICK

FEW people realize how tough a paper napkin is until they try to pull one apart which has been twisted up rope fashion. The performer can scarcely claim that this toughness is induced by means of magic, but after the spectators have tried to pull such a napkin in two and have failed in their efforts, the performer succeeds in doing so without exerting any effort at all.

The trick is done with the assistance of a little water. Before taking the napkin in his hands, the performer dips his fingers into a glass of water and takes the napkin by its center, holding it for a moment between his moistened fingers. The dampness is all that is needed to weaken the fibers of the napkin so that it will part in response to a gentle pull.

THE PHŒNIX RIBBON

THE magician shows a piece of tissue paper an inch wide and about six inches long. One third of the paper is red, one third white, and the remaining third blue. A match is touched to it, and it burns to ashes. Placing the ashes in his mouth, the magician draws forth many yards of red, white, and blue paper, which falls in a large heap at his feet.

The paper that is drawn from the mouth is prepared beforehand by pasting half-inch strips of differently colored paper end to end, until there is a strip eight or ten yards long. This strip is rolled up as tightly as possible, the outside end is pasted down, and the inside end is pulled out so that it can be gotten hold of easily.

The long strip is concealed in the performer's hand throughout the trick and is popped into his mouth when he pretends to put in the ashes of the original paper. As the long strip unrolls, it will seem to be endless, and there will be ample opportunity to drop the ashes to the floor behind it.

THE CONFETTI SHOWER

THE magician cuts a piece of tissue paper into small squares measuring about four inches to a side and dips these into a glass of water standing on his table. Taking the thoroughly soaked papers in one hand, he fans them with a fan held in the other hand, and a shower of dry confetti is wafted out of his hand and into the air. When his hand is opened, the wet papers have disappeared.

The confetti has, of course, been prepared beforehand and is wrapped in a piece of tissue paper, making a small packet. This packet is attached with wax or paste to the top of the under side of the fan which is lying open upon the table. After the papers have been dropped in the glass the performer picks up the fan with his right hand and casually rests his left hand on its top, thus removing the packet. He then lays down the fan and with his right hand picks the papers out of the glass and squeezes the moisture out of them placing them immediately afterward in his left hand. Picking up the fan with his right hand, he simultaneously breaks the tissue paper covering the confetti with his finger nails and then fans it out into the air. Under cover of the confetti shower, the wet papers are dropped to the floor.

THE PAPER AND KNIFE TRICK

THIS is an excellent little after-dinner trick, though it is also suitable for a regular "stage" performance. The performer cuts out six small squares of paper, moistens them, and sticks three of them to each side of a knife blade. He then tells his audience that there is a subtle intercommunication between the papers on each side of the blade, and they have a queer way of always acting together. Thus, if the center one, say, is removed from one side of the knife, the center one on the opposite side will also disappear. Suiting his actions to his words, he removes one of the center pieces and turns the knife over, when the opposite piece is seen to have vanished. The same process is repeated with the other two papers, and they are then all brought back again as at the start.

The trick depends for its effect upon a rapid twist of the knife, which makes it possible to show the audience the same side of the knife when they think they are seeing the opposite side. The knife is held between the thumb and forefinger, resting on the middle joint of the forefinger, pointing straight out in front of the performer and bent slightly downward, so that the audience can see the upper side of the blade. To show the opposite side, the hand is turned upward so that the knife points up in the air. When the first paper is removed, it is necessary to show the audience the same side of the knife again, and this is accomplished by turning the knife over while the hand is being brought up. The thumb pushes the knife toward the tip of the forefinger and rolls it over. The movement is reversed in bringing the knife down again. By this means the performer can show either side of the blade he pleases, and after a little practice the twist will be absolutely undetectable.

THE CUT–AND–RESTORED PAPER RIBBON

THERE are several methods of doing this trick, which is quite similar in effect to the cut-and-restored string trick, but the method here described is, in the opinion of many professionals, the very best and least known of all.

The performer shows a long red tissue-paper ribbon, folds it double, and snips off about an inch of the folded end with a pair of scissors. The ribbon is again folded and cut, and the process is continued until the entire ribbon has been cut into one-inch pieces. The performer gathers these up in one hand, seizes one of them with his other hand, and pulls out the ribbon restored to its original length.

Two duplicate ribbons are used, each about one inch wide and a yard long. One is folded up so that it makes a packet an inch square, and this packet is glued to one end of the other ribbon. It can be secured in place by gluing a small strip of similarly colored paper over it. When the ribbon has been cut as described, the performer still retains the prepared end in his hand, and it is placed on top of the pieces that have been cut off. At the first opportunity after displaying the restored ribbon, the cut pieces are gotten rid of, a good method being to wipe the face with a handkerchief and to secrete them in its folds before returning it to the pocket.

THE KNIFE–EDGED PAPER

A PENCIL and a dollar bill are borrowed from the audience, and one of the spectators is requested to hold the pencil by both ends. The performer folds the bill lengthwise and strikes the pencil with it two or three times. On the last stroke the pencil is broken cleanly in two, the edge of the bill apparently being sufficiently sharp to cut right through the wood.

The paper is not quite all that is needed to break the pencil, though, to all appearances, it does do so. On the last stroke, however, the performer extends his forefinger and strikes it fairly against the pencil as his arm descends. The pencil snaps in two, and the forefinger is instantly bent back into place.

THE COLORED PAPERS

A CHINA bowl is passed for examination, and the performer then produces four envelopes, each of which is filled with differently colored tissue paper clippings, one white, one red, one blue, and one yellow. The audience is asked to pour the clippings into the bowl, and the performer then asks which is the favorite of the four colors. Upon being told, he reaches into the bowl and brings out a handful of clippings of the chosen color. The other colors are named one by one, and the performer each time produces the color selected from the bowl.

The clippings used should be about an inch square, and before the performance the magician makes up four packets, each containing clippings of only one color. A piece of the same colored paper is passed around each packet and pasted in place to keep them from separating until the proper moment arrives. These four packets are concealed beneath the right side of the performer's vest, tucked lightly into the belt, and their order is remembered so that any color called for can be gotten hold of.

When asking the audience for their favorite color, the performer stands with his left side toward the spectators and his right hand, which is concealed from them by the body, resting on the packets, ready to pick out whichever one is chosen. The packet is concealed in the palm of the hand while the performer reaches into the bowl. He then breaks the tissue wrapper and drops the clippings back into the bowl a few at a time to create the impression of there being a great number of them.

THE FLOATING PAPER BALL

THE performer shows a paper napkin and rolls it into a ball, which he throws on the floor. At his word of command, however, it floats gracefully into the air and moves to and fro, the performer passing a hoop back and forth over it to prove that there are no strings or wires.

In reality there is a fine black thread which is attached to the wall or to a piece of furniture about six feet from the floor prior to the performance. A bent pin is attached to the other end and placed in a handy spot on the magician's table or fastened to the back of a chair by sticking the pin into the wood. The thread should stretch quite tightly between the two objects to which it is attached, and the napkin is rolled into a ball around it. When the napkin has been rolled up, the performer slacks away the thread so that it will fall to the floor, and the napkin is dropped to the floor. The performer now picks up the hoop, draws the pin and thread through it unobserved, and drops the hoop over his head and onto his shoulders. The pin is then calmly hooked into his coat lapel.

Now, by moving backward and forward, the ball can be made to rise into the air and float about, and the hoop can be removed from the shoulders and passed over it, since the thread already runs through its center.

THE COLORED NUMBER

TWO pieces of tissue paper, one red and the other blue, are placed on the table, and one of the spectators is then requested to select a cigarette paper from a pack and roll it into a small ball. The performer then asks the audience to choose one of the two colors, red or blue, and then to select a number between 1 and 1,000. When the cigarette paper is unrolled, the number is found written upon it in the chosen color.

The performer prepares for the trick by placing a packet of cigarette papers and a red and blue pencil in his right-hand coat pocket or trousers pocket. The red pencil is notched with a knife so that the performer can tell it from the blue one. When the color and number have been chosen, the performer writes the number with the proper pencil on the top sheet of the pack of papers in his pocket, removes it, and rolls it into a ball which he conceals between the tips of his forefinger and middle finger. The audience's paper is then taken in the left hand, picked up by the right hand, and tucked between the forefinger and middle finger, while the performer's paper is dropped into the palm of the left hand. This substitution is simplicity itself, if it is carefully practised a few times. The left hand is then extended so that the audience can take the paper and unroll it, the performer meanwhile dropping the other paper on the floor or into his pocket.

THE MARKED PAPER

THE magician produces a package of ordinary cigarette papers and asks the audience to select one. He then leaves the room while the selected paper is marked for identification. Upon his return the marked paper is mixed in with the rest of the package, the performer places them all behind his back and at once removes the marked paper.

The secret of this trick lies in the fact that practically all cigarette papers are cut on the bias, so that the corners are not exactly right angles. When the marked paper is pushed in between the others, which the performer retains in his possession throughout, he makes sure that it is inserted in the opposite way to those he is holding, so that two of its corners project beyond the other papers. When the papers are squared up, it is very easy to detect the projecting corners of the marked paper and withdraw it.

THE MAGNETIZED PAPERS

THE magician places four pieces of paper upon the back of his left hand and, with an air of mystery, blows them all off. He then replaces them and tells the spectators that he is able to induce magnetism into any of the pieces that he wishes; and to prove this he offers to blow away any one, two, or three of the pieces, retaining the other ones undisturbed in place by means of magnetism. When the audience choose which pieces they wish to remain in place, the performer places the fingers of his right hand upon them and blows the others away.

THE BENGAL BANDS

THE magician produces three loops of paper and gives one of them to a spectator together with a pair of scissors, requesting him to cut round the loop along the center line. When this has been done, the spectator has two separate loops, each of which is composed of paper one half the width of that in the original loop.

The performer then takes the scissors and cuts one of the remaining loops in the same way, but when he has finished, the two loops, instead of being separate, are interlinked. When he cuts the third loop, it comes out as a single loop with a diameter twice as great as that of the original loop.

The loops can be quickly made from strips of newspaper about four feet long and half an inch wide. The first loop is unprepared, but the second one is made by giving a half twist to the paper before pasting the ends together, and the third one is made by giving the paper two half twists.

THE GOOD-NIGHT PAPER TRICK

THIS startling effect is very good for the finale of a performance. Two pieces of tissue paper, one red and one white, are torn to pieces and rolled together into a ball. Presto! The ball is unrolled and the torn pieces are found to have arranged themselves so that the red paper spells out "Good-night" on the white paper.

Prior to the performance the letters which spell "Good-night" are cut out of red tissue paper and pasted on a piece of white tissue of the same size and shape as the piece that is to be torn. This prepared paper is rolled up in as small a ball as possible and placed on the table underneath the red and white pieces. When these are picked up, the prepared piece is picked up at the same time, being kept from sight behind the two other papers.

When the papers have been torn and rolled into a ball, they are held between the right thumb and forefinger, the prepared piece being gripped between the thumb and the base of the forefinger. The performer then pretends to place them in his left hand, but in reality drops the prepared piece in his left hand and tucks the torn pieces into the crotch of his thumb where the prepared piece was concealed. The prepared piece is then opened and shown to the audience. As soon as they have read the message on it, the performer crumples it up, at the same time wrapping the torn pieces in it, and tosses all of them onto the table or into a waste-paper basket.

STRING TRICKS AND ROPE TIES

THE CAPTIVES FREED

THE performer ties the two ends of a piece of string to the two wrists of one of the spectators then passes another string through the loop between the spectator's hands and requests someone to tie its ends around his wrists as shown in the diagram. The object is to disengage the two strings, thus freeing the two captives.

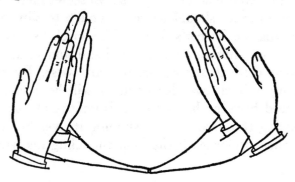

The performer does this by passing the bight, or central portion, of his string up through the loop encircling one of the spectator's wrists, over his hand, and down through the part of the loop at the back of his wrist. Then, by simply bringing the bight back up over the spectator's hand, the strings will be disengaged.

THE SLAVE BANGLE

A LARGE bracelet is borrowed from one of the ladies in the audience, and the performer then requests the spectators to tie his wrists together, leaving a foot or so of cord between the wrists. Taking the bracelet in his hand, he turns his back for an instant, and upon facing the audience again the bracelet is on the cord between his wrists. The string may be cut to remove the bracelet, or, if he so desires, the performer can turn his back and remove it in a matter of seconds by his own secret method.

The bracelet should be large enough to slip easily over the performer's hand. The trick is accomplished by slipping it over one hand and under the loop of cord that goes around his wrist. By then passing it back over his hand, it will be strung on the cord between his wrists. It is removed by simply reversing the process, first slipping it over his hand and then underneath the loop encircling his wrist.

LOOPING THE LOOP

THE performer removes his coat, hangs a long piece of string whose ends have been tied together over his right arm, and puts his right hand in his right vest pocket. The problem is to remove the string without taking the hand from the pocket.

It is accomplished as follows: Push the string through the right armhole of the vest, put the loop over your head, and then push it through the left armhole of the vest and put the left arm through it. The string now encircles the body, one strand of the loop passing across the back and the other across the chest. With the left hand it can be pulled down over the body to the feet, when the performer simply steps out of it.

THE SEVERED STRING

THIS is the old method of cutting and restoring a piece of string, and the trick that follows is a new version, so the two can be performed with good effect, one after the other.

Tie the two ends of a piece of string together, pass one hand through each end and give it a single twist. Then grasp the point at which the string crosses itself between the thumb and forefinger of the left hand and place both ends in the right hand, when the string will be linked, as shown in the diagram. Then cover the spot at which the strings are linked with the thumb and fingers of the left hand and grasp the string with the right hand a half an inch or so away from the link. One of the spectators is then asked to cut the section of string between your hands. In reality, he only cuts off a small

loop, and this is dropped unobserved to the floor
and the string exhibited restored to a single piece,
instead of being two pieces, as would naturally be
expected.

THE NEW CUT-AND-RESTORED STRING

IF THERE are any among your audience who are
familiar with the old version of the cut-and-
restored string, they will be very much puzzled when
you perform the trick in the new manner described
herewith.

A piece of string about a yard long is cut from a
ball of twine, and when the performer is cutting it
he secretly snips off a small piece about two inches
long, which he conceals in his right hand. If there is
time for preparation beforehand, this piece may be
cut off and placed in a handy pocket or in a convenient spot on the table.

In executing the trick, the performer takes an
end of the long string between the thumb and forefinger of each hand, allowing the center part to hang
loosely down. He then asks one of the spectators to
hand him the center part of the string, and when it
is given to him, he takes it between the second and
third fingers of each hand, the hands being held
about three inches apart. Now the performer releases
the portion of the string held between the second
and third fingers of the left hand, and with those
fingers takes the end piece held in the right hand, at

the same time shifting this end piece from between the thumb and forefinger to between the second and third fingers of the right hand. The string that passed between the right second and third fingers is dropped back into the palm of the right hand and held there. The short piece of string concealed in the right hand is then pushed up to take the place of the real end piece. Thus the right end piece is all that the spectator cuts.

After practising the motions a few times, they can be done practically instantaneously. The best way to cover the movement is to turn away slightly in order to point to the scissors, which should be on a table behind, or to one side of, the performer. When the string has been cut, the two short ends must be concealed in the palms of the hands until the string has been shown to be restored, when they can be thrown down on the table or put in a pocket together with the original string.

THE RELEASED CORD

THIS is one of the most deceptive little sleights in existence, and one that the audience can never do themselves, even though it looks easy.

The performer takes a piece of cord, or ribbon, about six inches long and ties the ends together. He then puts it on his forefingers, as shown in the diagram, and revolves his hands rapidly several times.

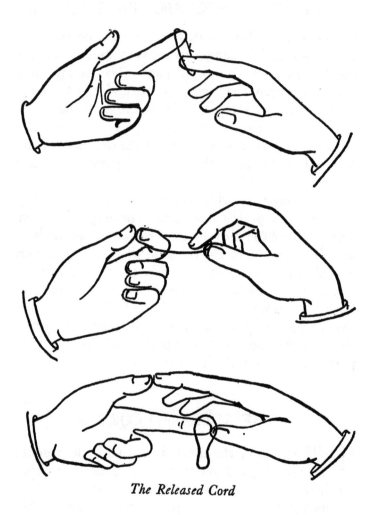

The Released Cord

He then places the forefinger of each hand upon the tip of the thumb of the same hand. The hands are now moved so that the right forefinger and the left thumb are uppermost, and then, by putting the end of the right forefinger against the tip of the left thumb, and the end of the left forefinger against the tip of the right thumb and raising the right forefinger and left thumb, the cord will be released and will fall to the ground.

The explanation is of necessity a trifle complicated, but by following it step by step the trick can be mastered in a few minutes.

THE STRING AND NOSE TRICK

TIE the two ends of a piece of string together and make a loop in one end, as shown in the diagram. In making the loop, hold a section of the string between the thumb and forefinger of each hand and double the right-hand part of the string over the left, being careful to make the right-hand part of the string the uppermost portion of the loop. Next place the loop between the teeth at the point marked A and insert the left forefinger at C, pulling the larger loop out taut.

Now insert the right forefinger from below upward in the loop B and bring it out to the right of the larger loop. Pass it over the right string of the larger loop and under the left string, and then place the tip of the right forefinger, which is still inserted in the little loop B, against the tip of the nose. Now, if you open your mouth and pull with the left hand,

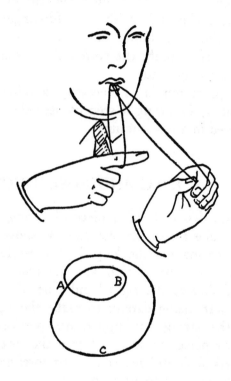

the string will pass right around your right forefinger, appearing as though it passed directly through it.

THE KEY AND STRING TRICK

THE two ends of a piece of string are tied together, a key or ring is threaded onto it, and the string is then looped over one of the spectator's thumbs. The magician then proceeds to remove the key without taking the string from the spectator's thumbs.

In order to remove the key, the performer takes the string which is on the side nearest the spectator's body, grasping it to the right of the key. He then loops it over the spectator's right thumb, being careful to start the loop on the side toward the spectator. Now, if the loop which was originally around the spectator's right thumb is slipped off, the key will be released and will fall to the ground.

THE SCISSORS AND STRING TRICK

THIS is another trick on the same order as the one last described, but the method employed in effecting the release is slightly different.

A doubled piece of string is threaded through the handles of a pair of scissors, as shown in the diagram, and the opposite end is given to a member of the audience to hold. To remove the scissors from the string, the performer takes the loop end of the string fastened to the lower handle of the scissors and passes it through the upper handle and around

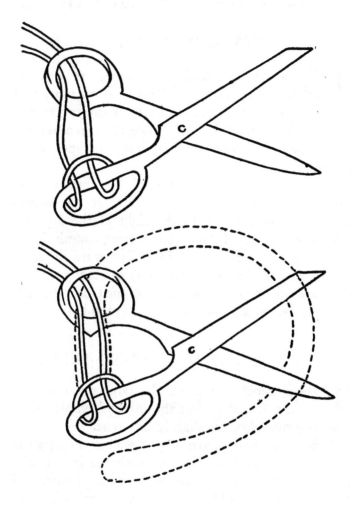

The Scissors and String Trick

the blades as indicated by the dotted line. The string will then slip right through the handles of the scissors.

THE BUTTONHOLE AND STRING TRICK

THE performer takes a piece of string, ties the two ends together, and passes it through a buttonhole in his coat, hooking his thumbs in the loops at each end. With a sudden movement, the string is freed from the buttonhole, although the two thumbs are still in place and have, apparently, never been removed.

The trick is done as follows: The thumbs should be passed through the loops at each end of the string from the bottom upward. The little finger of the right hand is then hooked under the string which is nearest to it of the two strings running from the left thumb to the buttonhole. The left little finger is similarly hooked in the corresponding string running from the right thumb to the buttonhole. The right thumb is then slipped out of its loop and put through the loop held by the right little finger, which is drawn well over to the right to facilitate the movement. As the thumb is inserted, the right little finger is withdrawn. Now the left little finger releases the string around which it is crooked, the thumbs are rapidly drawn apart, and the string comes free of the buttonhole, appearing as though it had been pulled right through the fabric of the coat.

THE PAPER AND BUTTON TRICK

THIS is a puzzle rather than a trick, but it can be quickly made when the magician is called upon to show his knowledge of the mystifying and, like most puzzles, is extremely hard to solve unless you know how.

Take a piece of thick paper about three by six inches in size and cut two slits in it lengthwise, each slit being about three inches long and the distance between them half an inch. About half an inch be-

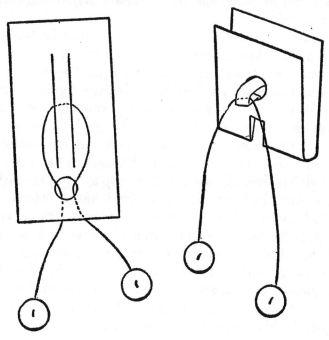

low the slits cut a circular hole slightly more than half an inch in diameter. Then pass a string between the slits and through the hole, as shown in the diagram, and to its ends attach two buttons or two circular pieces of cardboard having a diameter of an inch or more.

The problem is to remove the string which, apparently, can only be accomplished by passing the buttons through the much smaller hole. After the audience has tried and failed, the magician succeeds as follows. The string is first seized at the place where it passes in back of the strip of paper between the two slits and is pulled upward until the loop it forms is about halfway to the top of the slits. The strip of paper and the loop of string are then pulled forward toward the performer, and the paper is bent and passed backward through the small hole. Then, by simply passing one of the buttons through the loop formed by the strip of paper projecting through the hole, the buttons and string will both be freed.

THE YARKAND ROPE ESCAPE

THE performer's wrists are tied tightly together with a handkerchief, and a length of rope is passed between them, the two ends being held by a member of the audience. In less than no time the performer has miraculously freed himself from the rope.

The trick is done as follows. The performer takes care not to let his wrists be tied too tightly, as he needs a little working room in between them. The first move in releasing the rope is to work the bight, or loop, which passes in back of the handkerchief, up between the palms of the hands. When this is done, he simply passes his right hand through the loop, and the rope slides off between his wrist and the handkerchief.

THE IMPROMPTU THUMB TIE

THERE is a very famous thumb-tie trick which is performed by many prominent magicians on the professional stage, but since it requires apparatus it is outside the scope of the present volume. The trick described herewith, however, is every bit as effective and has the added virtue of being easy to perform at any time and at any place without preparation of any sort.

The performer allows his thumbs to be tied tightly together with a strong piece of cord or a tape, and he then succeeds in instantly releasing them, slipping his arm through that of a person standing beside him, or looping a hoop over his arm, yet when his hands are reunited his thumbs are as tightly tied as at first.

The trick is done as follows: Hold your hands palm upward in front of you with the string to be used for tying the thumbs lying across them, passing across the palms, but between the first finger and thumb of each hand. Then bring your hands together, bending in the fingers toward the wrists, and as you do so catch the middle part of the string between the fourth and fifth fingers of each hand. Now your thumbs can be tied together as tightly as possible, yet they can be extricated instantly by simply opening the fingers, thereby leaving a large loop of string between your hands, out of which the thumbs can be drawn at will. When reuniting the hands, put the thumb which was withdrawn inside the loop, catch the bottom of the loop between the fourth and fifth fingers of each hand, and everything will appear to be as tightly tied as before.

THE EXCELSIOR ROPE TIE

THIS is one of the most famous of all rope ties and one which has been used repeatedly in professional "spiritualistic" demonstrations.

Two ropes are passed for examination and are then tied to the performer's wrists, the end of one rope being tied around one wrist and the end of the other rope around the other wrist. The performer then sits in a chair and crosses his arms, and the ends of the ropes are fastened to the rungs of the chair. A screen is placed in front of him, and he immediately commences to ring bells which have been left by the chair, clap his hands, write messages on slates or paper, toss objects over the screen, and perform other "spiritual" feats. Nevertheless, when the screen is removed, he is still tightly bound as before.

A little experimenting will show that it is very simple partially to extricate one's self from the rope tie described. By sliding to the front edge of the chair and lifting either arm over the head, it is possible to get up and have considerable freedom of movement. At the conclusion of the demonstration, the performer slips back into his original position, and it appears as though he had never moved from it.

THE STRANGLE ROPE TIE

IN THIS rope tie a length of rope is passed beneath the performer's right leg a little above the knee and drawn through until the ends are of equal length on each side. One of the spectators then knots the rope over the performer's leg and ties his right wrist securely on top of the knot. The left wrist is then bound on top of the right wrist, the performer bends forward, and the ropes are passed around his neck, and his head is tied down to his wrists. Within a few moments after a screen is placed in front of him, the performer makes his escape.

The weak point of the tie, and that which enables the performer to free himself so rapidly, is the fact that the first knot tied is only a single knot, which experiment will show can be made to slip along the rope. While he is being bound, the performer sits near the front edge of the chair with both feet on the rungs, and this expands his leg muscles to such an extent that, when he straightens out his leg, there will be quite a little bit of slack between his leg and the rope. The single knot is worked down on this slack part of the rope until the right hand is freed, and the other knots can then be untied.

THE KELLAR ROPE TIE

THIS is the tie made famous by Harry Kellar, the great magician, and it is worthy in every respect to bear his name. The audience first ties the center of a length of rope around the performer's left wrist. He puts his left hand behind his back, places his right wrist over the knot on his left wrist, and the audience then bind his two wrists firmly together. In an instant the performer can free himself and do spiritualistic stunts or whatever he pleases, yet he is bound as securely as ever when the demonstration comes to an end.

The left wrist must be tied so that the knot comes on the inside of the wrist. When the performer puts his hands behind his back, he grasps one of the ends of the rope with his right hand and quickly makes a loop around the knot already tied. This loop is covered right away by the right wrist which presses

firmly against it while his wrists are being bound together. No matter how tight the knots may be, the
right hand can instantly be slipped out of the loop.
In replacing the hands, the left hand grasps the slack
part of the loop and twists it into its original position around the knot.

MIND READING, SECOND SIGHT, AND SPIRIT TRICKS

THE QUICK OR THE DEAD

THE performer tears a piece of notepaper into five strips and hands them to a member of the audience with the request that he first write the names of two dead people—presidents, kings, or whoever he wishes—and then the names of three living people. The slips are folded with the writing inside and placed on a table or in a hat. The performer at once picks out the slips containing the names of the dead people or, as a variation, he asks the audience which they wish him to select, the quick or the dead, and picks out whichever is selected.

In tearing the paper, the performer uses a ruler so that all five strips will have straight edges and appear identical in size and shape. The top and bottom strips, however, can always be told from the other three as one of each of their edges will be machine cut and will be smoother than the other edge. These two strips are placed on top of the others and the spectator, of course, writes the names of dead people upon them.

The trick can also be done by giving one slip apiece to five different members of the audience and requesting the two persons who have the top and bottom slips to write the names of dead people, while the other three write the names of people still living.

THE MYSTERIOUS TOTAL

A PIECE of blank paper is given to the audience, and six people are requested to write any number they wish between 1 and 10. After each person has written his number he folds the paper down so that the next person cannot see what has been written, thus precluding the possibility of a confederate reading the numbers and signaling the total to the performer. After all the numbers have been written, the folded paper is enclosed in another larger piece of paper, which is folded and fastened with glue or sealing wax. The performer instantly announces the total of the hidden numbers which proves to be correct when the large paper is unfolded, the slip removed, and the numbers added up.

In preparing for this trick the performer folds two large pieces of notepaper, first folding in the top and bottom and then folding over the two sides. The papers are then glued together back to back in the folded position. On a smaller piece of paper, identical with that which is later given to the audience, the performer writes any six numbers between 1 and 10 and memorizes their total. This slip is folded, as the audience are later instructed to fold theirs, and is placed in one side of the large paper which is folded up and sealed with glue or sealing wax, whichever the performer intends to use.

The audience's slip is, of course, wrapped up in

the other side of the double paper, but in opening this paper the performer reverses it and removes his own slip.

THE CHOSEN NUMBER

THIS is a novelty in mind-reading experiments and will be found particularly useful with a skeptical audience who think that some verbal, or other kind of code, must be used to transmit messages telepathically. In this trick the performer is blindfolded and led from the room while the audience selects a number. The performer then returns and places his hand on his assistant's forehead in order to receive the thought waves more readily. No word is spoken, yet the performer quickly announces the chosen number.

The means of transmission employed to get the number across to the performer is exceptionally clever and one that the audience would never dream of. The assistant simply puts his teeth together and clamps his jaw the proper number of times to indicate the figures making up the number. The performer, with his hand on the assistant's temple, can feel the movements of the bone.

To indicate zero the jaw must be clamped ten times. Thus the number ten would be indicated by one clamp, then a short wait, and then ten clamps in succession. With a few moment's practice, the assistant will discover just how to place his upper and lower teeth so no outward movement will be visible while he is signaling.

THE BLINDFOLD SECOND-SIGHT ACT

IN THIS method of performing second sight, the "medium" is blindfolded and seated in a chair facing the audience. The performer then writes on a blackboard the names of cards chosen by the audience, columns of figures, the names of articles collected from the audience, and so on. The medium, without being spoken to, calls out whatever card or object has been written down, adds up the figures, answers questions, etc.

In blindfolding his assistant the performer is careful to do so in such a way that he can see down under the handkerchief into his lap. Concealed in his hand, the assistant carries a little mirror, and in this he can see reflected whatever is written on the blackboard, which is placed some distance to one side and a little in back of him. If a blackboard is unobtainable, a large sheet of paper may be hung against the wall and the questions, etc., written on it in a bold hand.

The ostensible purpose of the blackboard is, of course, to acquaint the entire audience with the object to be named without making it necessary for the performer even to whisper it. Naturally, the more silently the act is carried out, the more mysterious it seems.

WHICH OBJECT?

SEVERAL objects of a different nature, such as a match box, a book, an ink bottle, etc., are placed on a table, and while the performer leaves the room the audience selects one of them. Upon his return, the performer at once tells which of the objects was selected.

In this trick an assistant is used who indicates the chosen object by means of a simple code, so simple, in fact, that it is all the harder to guess. Four objects are generally used and, if possible, should be placed in a row. The magician and his assistant assign to each a number, the one on the left end of the row, for example, always being Number One, the next object Number Two, and so on.

To indicate that Number One has been chosen, the assistant addresses the performer with a sentence commencing with a one-letter word such as "*I* think you will have a hard time guessing this." To indicate Number Two the first word of the sentence should contain two letters, for example: "*Do* you think you can guess it?" For Number Three he can say: "*Can* you guess it?" or "*You* will have a hard time guessing it," and for Number Four such a sentence as: "*Don't* be too sure now; this is a hard one," or "*What* do you think was chosen?" will speedily tell the performer which object was chosen. The sentences can be varied almost indefinitely, thus throwing the audience off the scent.

THE BANK-NOTE MIND READER

THE magician seats himself at one side of the room, or stage, and his assistant borrows several bank notes from the audience. He does not go near the magician, but holds the notes up one by one, and the performer at once calls out the serial numbers printed thereon.

The explanation of the trick lies in the use of a very clever and undetectable finger code. The numbers from zero to 9 are indicated as follows:

Zero—The assistant holds the bill by the top edge.

1—The assistant holds the bill in his right hand with the thumb in back and the forefinger slightly extended across the face of the bill.

2—The bill is held in the same way as for the number 1 but the first and second fingers are extended.

3—Same as before but with three fingers extended.

4—Same as before but with all four fingers extended.

5—The assistant holds the bill by the bottom edge.

6—The assistant holds the bill in his left hand with the forefinger extended across the face.

7—Same as for the number 6, but the first and second fingers are extended.

8—Same as before but with three fingers extended.

9—Same as before but with all four fingers extended.

SECOND SIGHT

THE second-sight trick described herewith is one of the most baffling of all such tricks and has been used on the vaudeville stage by professional mind readers with great success. The audience are furnished with a number of slips of paper upon which they are asked to write whatever they please, such as names, dates, messages, and so on. The slips are then folded over and collected, and the performer selects one, places it against his forehead, concentrates deeply, and then announces what is written on the paper, repeating this with the remaining slips.

The secret of the trick lies in the use of a confederate with whom the mind reader has previously come to an understanding. The confederate, for example, will write "George Washington" on his slip of paper, and before the slips are collected marks his own with a small cross so that the performer can identify it. When the slips have been collected and placed on the performer's table, he picks one out at random and announces that it contains the words "George Washington." He then asks if anyone in the audience wrote these words, and the confederate replies in the affirmative. There then being no question of the performer's powers, he unfolds the slip which is in his hand and reads what is written on it at the same time pretending that he is merely confirming the correctness of his reading by repeating "George Washington; yes, that is correct."

Having read what was on the slip which was, say, the date 1492, he selects another slip, holds it to his forehead, and announces that he can see the date 1492 written on it. The process is repeated until all the slips have been read, care being taken to leave the confederate's slip till the very last.

CHESS EXTRAORDINARY

IF YOU play chess you are, no doubt, familiar with what is known as the knight's move, which consists of moving the knight either two squares in one direction and then one square in a direction at right angles to the first move, or else one square in one direction and then two squares at right angles to the direction of the first move. This move, which should be explained to the audience, is the basis of the following exceptionally effective "memory feat."

The magician rules off a large sheet of paper into sixty-four squares to represent a chess board, and numbers the squares from 1 to 64, starting at the upper left-hand corner and numbering from left to right. Thus the topmost row would read 1—2—3—4—5—6—7—8, and the bottom row would read 57—58—59—60—61—62—63—64. He then asks the audience to select any square they wish and tells them that he proposes to start with the knight on that square and, using only the knight's move described above, to traverse the entire chess board touching every square once only and finally returning to the square from which he started, a feat which seemingly calls for a master mind and extraordinary powers of memory and concentration.

One of the spectators is given a pencil, and when the square from which the knight is to commence his journey has been selected, the performer goes to another part of the room, turns his back upon the impromptu chess board, and commences to call out the numbers of the squares to which the knight is to move. As he calls out each square, the spectator draws a line to it with his pencil, so that a complete diagram of all the moves will be obtained which can subsequently be checked to make sure that no squares were missed or visited twice.

To do this trick the magician must provide himself with a key consisting of the numbers from 1 to 64 written out on the back of a visiting card in the following order: 1—11—5—15—32—22—39—56—62—45—60—50—33—43—26—9—3—20—14—8—23—29—12—2—19—25—35—41—58—52—37—47—64—54—44—59—49—34—17—27—10—4—21—6—16—31—48—38—55—61—51—57—42—36—53—63—46—40—30—24—7—13—28—18.

Now, supposing that the audience wishes the moves to commence from square 19, the performer steps to the other side of the room, turns his back, and secretly takes the key from his vest pocket. Retaining it in his right hand, he folds his arms and bows his head as if in deep concentration. In this position, he can easily see the key, and all he has to do is to read the numbers one after the other, the audience meanwhile following the moves with the pencil. When the end or number 18 is reached, he goes back to number 1 and reads along until number 19, the starting point, is reached, when it will be found that he has fulfilled his promise and covered the entire board, always using the knight's move and touching each square only once.

THE SPIRIT SLATE

THE spirits that do the performer's bidding in the accomplishment of this trick are very rapid workers. No cabinet is used, nor is there delay of any kind while the message is being written. The performer holds the slate in his hand, shows it back and front, and before the very eyes of the audience a mysterious message is written on it.

Prior to the performance, the magician writes any message he pleases on the slate, and the side that contains the writing is then covered with a piece of slate-colored cloth. A visit to a dry-goods store will be rewarded with several kinds of cloth that will be suitable. The cloth is stretched tight and held in place with little pieces of wax. Attached to one cor-

ner of the cloth is a black thread which leads up the
performer's sleeve, across his back, and down the
other sleeve to the wrist, around which it is knotted.
To make the writing appear, the performer extends
the hand which is holding the slate thus increasing
the tension on the thread and whisking the cloth up
the sleeve.

THE SPIRIT MESSAGE

THE audience are requested to write the names
of some of our presidents on pieces of paper
which are furnished by the performer. The papers
are folded and put in a hat, and one is selected and
given to a spectator to hold. The remaining papers
are burned, and the performer rubs their ashes
upon his forearm, when the name of the President
on the selected paper appears in black letters on his
arm.

Before the performance the performer writes the
name of a prominent President, such as Lincoln
or Washington, on his forearm with a piece of soap.
He writes the same name on a number of pieces
of paper similar to those which are furnished to
the audience. The prepared slips are encircled with
a rubber band and concealed beneath the lower edge
of the vest. After collecting the audience's slips, the
performer returns to his table for a hat or box in
which to place them, and while his back is turned to

the audience he gets the prepared slips in his hand and drops them into the hat. The audience's slips are dropped behind a box or other object on the table or put into the performer's pocket at the first opportunity.

When the ashes of the unchosen slips are rubbed over the performer's forearm, they will cling to the soap and form the name of the chosen President.

SPIRIT WRITING

AN ORDINARY slate is given for examination and is washed on both sides with a sponge. It is then wrapped in a piece of newspaper so that no human hands can touch it, and, to make assurance doubly sure, it is placed on a chair, and one of the spectators is requested to sit on it. Despite these precautions, however, it is found that a ghostly hand has written a message on the slate when the newspaper is removed.

The message is previously written backward on the newspaper with a piece of chalk. In wrapping up the slate the performer is careful to place the writing next to one side of the slate. The spectator is, of course, requested to sit on it so that the writing will be transferred with the help of his weight, though the reason given by the performer is that it is an extra precaution against substitution or trickery of any sort.

THE THIRSTY SPIRITS

THIS is a novel "test" to use in connection with rope ties and other "spiritualistic" forms of magic in which the performer, bound and helpless, summons the departed to do his bidding. A glass of water is carefully covered with adhesive tape so that it is impossible for anyone to drink from it. The performer is tied and placed behind a screen together with the glass. When the screen is removed, the water has disappeared, though the tape is undisturbed in any way.

The secret lies in the fact that the performer has a drinking straw in one of his pockets. This is inserted between the strips of tape, and the water is vanished in what is, after all, a very normal manner.

THE NUMBER, COIN, AND BOOK TRICK

THIS is a combination mind-reading feat which seems much more complicated than it really is. The magician requests a member of the audience to write a three-figure number on a piece of paper, to reverse it, and subtract the smaller from the larger number. He then asks another member of the audience to take a coin from his pocket and write the date on a piece of paper. The magician then takes a book, opens it, asks the spectator to put the paper with the coin's date on it between the pages at which it is opened, and to hold the book until it is needed.

The first spectator is then asked to add together the figures that he obtained as a result of his subtraction, and the second spectator is asked to add together the figures that make up the date on the coin. These two totals are added, and the book is opened at the page where the paper was inserted. The number of the page is the same number arrived at by the audience's computations.

The secret of the trick lies in the fact that when the first spectator adds together the figures obtained by his subtraction, he will always obtain 18, no matter what original number he wrote down. For example, suppose he wrote 674. His calculation would be as follows:

$$\begin{array}{r} 674 \\ -476 \\ \hline 198 \end{array}$$

Adding 1, 9, and 8, the total is 18.

While the second spectator is writing down the date on the coin, the performer catches a glimpse of the paper, notes the date, adds its figures together, and adds their total to 18. Suppose the date was 1915. The total of the individual figures would be 16, which added to 18, makes 34. He accordingly casually opens the book to page 34 and has the owner of the coin put his paper in at this point.

THE SPIRITS' ANSWER

THE magician shows a small writing tablet, inserts a piece of carbon paper between the first and second sheets, and asks one of the spectators to write a question on the top sheet, signing his name beneath it. As soon as this is done, the magician removes the carbon paper and asks the spectator to look at the second sheet. There, written just above the carbon copy of his signature, is a spirit answer to his question.

The writing tablet used should be the kind that has perforations at the top so that the sheets tear off easily. It is prepared before the performance as follows: Lift up the three top sheets of paper and lay a piece of carbon paper on top of the fourth sheet. On top of the carbon place a loose sheet of paper, and on this paper write a "spirit answer" worded so as to form an answer to any question. Examples are: "It will not be long before you know what you are seeking"; "The stars favor you but you must be careful," or "The spirits are helping you and you will soon hear from them."

Remove the carbon paper and the loose sheet of paper and "dog-ear" the corners of the third and fourth sheets of the tablet, so that they can be handled as a single sheet. Now cut a piece of carbon paper the same width as the tablet but one third again as long and fold it over so that only one third of the shiny under side is exposed.

In presenting the effect, show the tablet to the audience and place the prepared piece of carbon paper between the first two sheets, being careful to have the single thickness, that is, the part with the shiny surface exposed, toward the top. Write the magical word "Abracadabra" on the first sheet near the top, tear the paper off, and show the audience the carbon copy of the word on the second sheet. Everything is plain and aboveboard, so tear off the second sheet and discard it.

Now lift up the third and fourth sheets together by means of the "dog-eared" corners and show the audience that the sheet underneath is perfectly blank. Take the carbon paper and insert it between the third and fourth sheets, separating their corners for this purpose. In doing this, make sure that the carbon paper is turned around so that the doubled-over end is toward the top of the tablet and the single thickness is toward the bottom, right under where the spectator will sign his name, as a matter of fact.

Ask a spectator to write a question at the top of the paper and sign his name at the bottom. The doubled-over part of the carbon paper at the top will prevent a carbon copy of the question being made on the under sheet, but there will be a copy of the signature. Take the pad back, remove the carbon paper, and give the pad back to the spectator, requesting him to see if the spirits have answered his question. When he looks on the under sheet of paper, he will find the answer where the copy of his question should be, and underneath it his own signature.

THE FAMOUS BOOK TEST

IN THIS exceedingly baffling mind-reading trick, the performer uses an assistant who sits in full view of the audience but with his back turned toward them. The audience is requested to choose any book they wish from those in the room or in any near-by room. The book is opened at any page desired, and any paragraph on that page is selected and read over silently. The book is then closed and handed to the assistant. After a few moments of concentration, he opens the book and reads the paragraph which was selected.

All that is needed to perform this effect is a small pasteboard card, such as a visiting card, and a short pencil stub. Both card and pencil are placed in the performer's right-hand trouser pocket prior to the performance, and while the selected paragraph is being read by the spectator, the performer puts his hand in his pocket and writes the number of the page and the number of the paragraph on the page. When the spectator closes the book, the performer takes it in his left hand and immediately afterward transfers it to his right hand, which he has withdrawn from his pocket, bringing along the card. Both card and book are handed to the assistant, without a word being exchanged, and a moment later the assistant reads the chosen paragraph, having, to all appearances, discovered it by means of mental telepathy.

WHEN THE SPIRITS WHISPER

AT THE performer's request, three spectators draw cards from the deck and place them on top of the deck without looking at them. The three cards are immediately dealt off onto the table face downward, and another spectator is asked to select one of them. The chosen card is shown to the audience, and one of the spectators is then requested to take a pencil and piece of paper to the magician's assistant, who has been in another room during the first part of the trick. As soon as the assistant receives the pencil, he writes the name of the chosen card, which, according to the magician, has been whispered in his ear by a spirit messenger.

The effect is worked as follows. Before the performance, the magician turns a half-dozen cards on the bottom of the pack face upward, and on top of these he places three cards which his assistant has memorized, knowing their names and also the order in which they are arranged. The three cards which the spectators select are placed on the top of the pack, which is then reversed so that the three prearranged cards are on the top. These are dealt off onto the table, and any one of them is chosen by the audience.

In his pocket the magician has three pencils, one short, one medium length, and the other full length. The chosen card is indicated to the assistant by the pencil brought out to him by one of the audience, the pencil used being, of course, one of the three in the magician's pocket. The short pencil indicates the first of the three prearranged cards, the medium-length pencil the second card, and the full-length pencil the third card.

TRICKS WITH GLASSES

THE MYSTIC GLASS

WHATEVER is put into the mystic glass mysteriously disappears immediately afterward. The secret lies in the use of an invisible hair net which the performer drops into the glass, allowing the edge to hang over the top. Anything that is dropped into the glass will now fall into the net. The glass is covered with a handkerchief, and when it is removed the net is lifted with it, bringing along the coin, match box, or whatever else was dropped into the glass.

THE VANISHING GLASS

THIS is one of the best of all after-dinner tricks and one that is extremely mystifying to the uninitiated. The magician puts a small piece of bread on the table and covers it with an inverted drinking glass. He then covers the glass with a piece of newspaper or wrapping paper, pressing it tightly, so that it is shaped to the glass.

His object is, apparently, to make the bread disappear, yet when he lifts the glass it is still there. A second time he replaces and removes the glass, yet the bread is still on the table.

"Well," says the magician, "this time there will be no doubt about it: the bread will positively vanish," and he picks it up and eats it. Upon picking up the paper, it is found that the glass has also mysteriously disappeared, only to be found a moment later in a sideboard drawer or in someone's coat pocket.

The first time the glass is replaced over the bread, everything is as it should be, but the second time the magician removes the glass he moves it over to the edge of the table while he is centering attention on the bread, and allows the glass to drop into his lap. The paper still retains its cylindrical shape and when it is put back on the table it still looks as though the glass were inside it. As he lifts the paper and reveals the disappearance of the glass, he pushes it up under his vest where it can remain safely hidden until the moment arrives for revealing it in some unexpected place.

THE BALANCED GLASS

THIS is a good after-dinner trick which exhibits to good advantage the magician's uncanny power of making inanimate objects obey his commands. The trick consists in balancing a drinking glass half full of water on its edge so that it inclines at an angle of nearly forty-five degrees.

The trick is done by putting a match under the

tablecloth, which must be done unobserved. By resting the bottom of the glass against the match and exercising a little care in doing so, it can be made to balance very nicely.

BLOWING THROUGH A GLASS

THE performer lights a candle, places it on the table, and then puts a glass between the candle and himself. These preparations should be made with an air of mystery, and a great pretense should be made of putting the glass in exactly the right spot, moving it backward and forward a few times with an air of intense concentration.

The performer then blows against the glass, and the candle is at once extinguished, the air having apparently passed right through the glass. In reality, if one blows against the center of the glass, the air currents divide and reunite on the opposite side of the glass, striking the flame with all of their original strength.

THE GLASS AND PLATE BALANCE

AS A bit of after-dinner juggling, this trick is unsurpassed. The magician places a drinking glass on the edge of a plate held in his hand and succeeds in balancing it for a considerable time before it finally falls off.

The thumb of the hand that holds the plate is the factor which, unknown to the audience, makes the trick possible. The plate is held so that the fingers are in front of it and the thumb behind, and by resting the rear portion of the bottom of the glass on the end of the thumb, the balance can be easily achieved.

THE INVERTED GLASS

THE magician fills a glass with water, places it upon the table, and rests another glass, which is empty, mouth downward on the rim of the first glass trick. The trick is to remove the upper glass and drink the water in the lower glass without touching either of them with the hands.

This is accomplished by removing the upper glass between the chin and the neck and holding it in this position while the lower glass is drawn to the edge of the table with the teeth and tipped over until the water can be reached and swallowed.

THE BALANCED GLASSES

THIS feat is also a demonstration of how the magician can achieve the impossible without the use of his hands.

A wineglass is partially filled with water, and another wineglass is inverted and rested on top of it. The problem is to pour the water contained in the lower glass into the upper glass without touching the upper glass with the hands.

The magician does this by bending over the glasses and taking the further side of the bottom of the upper glass in his teeth. When he raises his head, the upper glass will be held upright between his teeth, and it is then a simple matter to pour into it the water contained in the other glass.

MISCELLANEOUS TRICKS

ADAM'S APPLE

AN APPLE is selected by the audience from a dish of fruit, and the magician threads it on two pieces of tape which are attached to a large needle. The tapes are knotted over the apple, and the ends are given to two spectators. Covering the apple with a handkerchief, the magician reaches under it and, in a moment, removes the apple from the tapes.

The tapes, which should be about three feet long, are prepared before the performance by doubling each one back on itself and sewing the looped ends together with fine white thread. They are then threaded on a large needle, rolled up, and placed in a convenient spot on the magician's table.

In showing the trick, pass the needle and tapes through the center of the apple, drawing them through until the point where the tapes are joined together is hidden inside the apple. Then ask two spectators to hold the tapes, one being given the ends which project from one side of the apple, and the second spectator the tapes projecting from the opposite side. Each spectator is thus holding the two ends of one piece of tape and, for the trick to succeed, it is necessary to give each of them an end of each of the tapes. This is accomplished by taking one end from each spectator and tying them in a single knot over the apple, as shown in the diagram,

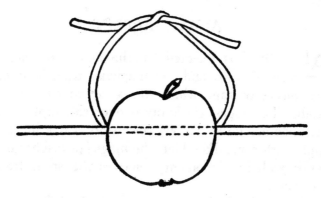

thus giving each spectator the end formerly held by the other one.

A handkerchief is then thrown over the apple and under cover of its folds the magician gives the apple a sharp jerk, which releases it from the tapes.

THE CUT–AND–RESTORED TAPES

THIS is a comparatively little known method of cutting and magically restoring two ribbons or tapes. The tapes are cut in the middle of their length, and the four severed ends are shown the audience. The performer lights the ends with a match, rubs them between his hands, and exhibits the tapes entirely restored to their original length.

Two pieces of ordinary white tape of equal length are cut from a roll and folded double, so that one end of each forms a loop. The two loop ends are joined together by two pieces of tape about an inch long. These tapes can be fastened to the larger ones with paste, which will hold firmly yet will leave no visible trace. The performer cuts through the small tapes, thus leaving the large tapes unharmed. The short ends are burned down and rubbed off between the hands before exhibiting the large tapes in their restored condition.

THE SELF-STARTING ROLLING BALL

THE magician places a small ball on the table, which may be either his professional table or a dinner table, and causes it to roll across the table of its own accord. It is a most mysterious effect.

The trick is accomplished by having a small ring with a thread attached to it secreted beneath the tablecloth. The ball is placed on the ring, and when the performer pulls on the thread, the ball starts to roll in the most unaccountable manner.

The trick can be made more effective by having the ball roll away from the performer, and this can be accomplished by leading the thread from the ring to the opposite side of the table to that at which the performer is seated, and then back underneath the table.

THE FLYING BALL

THIS is a trick that has frequently been elaborately presented on the professional stage but that is excellently adapted for parlor or club use. The magician holds in his hand a small ball. Suddenly it leaves his hand and travels through the air to his other hand. From here it flies slowly but surely across the stage and out of sight.

If it is simply desired to make the ball travel from hand to hand, a loop of thread about a yard long should be used, one end being looped over each hand. The ball travels along between the parallel strands of thread. If the ball is to fly across the stage, one end of the loop should be fastened off stage and the opposite end looped over the performer's hand.

THE COIN, HANDKERCHIEF, AND RING TRICK

A HANDKERCHIEF is spread out on the table, and a coin is placed in its center. The four corners of the handkerchief are then gathered up and passed through a ring, which is drawn down over the handkerchief until it rests on top of the coin. The handkerchief is next placed on the table, the corners are opened out, and two spectators are requested to put their hands on the corners and to hold them firmly against the table. Another handkerchief is then thrown over all, and under its cover the magician extracts both the coin and ring from the first handkerchief, despite the fact that the corners held by the spectators are never moved or disturbed.

The trick is made possible by a little unobtrusive "fixing" of the handkerchief as it lies on the table. Two of its corners are brought as close together as is possible without attracting attention. To extract the coin, the performer takes the side of the handkerchief which is between these two corners and works it through the ring. There will be plenty of slack to do this without moving the corners held by the spectators, though at first glance it seems impossible. When the edge of the handkerchief has been pushed through the ring, the coin can be extracted and the ring will then slip off the handkerchief.

THE RIBBON AND ORANGE TRICK

THIS trick may be performed either as an after-dinner stunt or as part of a regular programme. It makes use of a new principle, which is very interesting and clever. In effect, the magician takes an orange which the audience has selected and, cutting it open, draws forth a long piece of ribbon.

The orange used should be a tangerine or a small-sized ordinary orange. The ribbon is threaded through a large needle and then wound tightly around the needle, its outer end being glued down. When showing the trick, the performer secretes the ribbon and needle in his left hand and places the orange on top of it, pushing down so that the needle will penetrate right through the orange. The top of the orange is then cut away around the needle, and the ribbon is drawn right through the orange.

THE AMBULATING EGG

THE performer gives an egg to be examined and borrows two hats from the audience. Returning to his table, he places the egg in one of the hats. It immediately climbs up the inside of the hat, moves across the brim, and drops down into the other hat which is held so that its brim touches that of the first hat. At the magician's command, it walks back and forth in this manner as long as desired, and, at any moment, it can be picked up and handed for examination.

The secret lies in the use of a piece of black thread about twelve to fifteen inches long. One end is fastened to one of the performer's vest buttons and the other end is knotted through a small piece of adhesive tape. While returning to his table with the egg in his hand, the performer presses the adhesive tape firmly against it. After the egg has been dropped into the hat, the performer makes it climb out and move back and forth by slightly twisting his body.

PUTTING AN EGG INTO A BOTTLE

A HARD–BOILED egg is considerably larger than the mouth of a pint milk bottle, and, by ordinary means, at least, it is impossible to force it inside the bottle. The magician, however, is always ready to make the impossible possible, and the case in point is no exception.

After the audience have tried every way they can think of to insert the egg through the mouth of the bottle, the magician lights a small piece of paper, puts it inside the bottle, and places the egg on top of the bottle. Almost instantly the vacuum created by the flaming paper draws the egg through the mouth of the bottle. The eggshell should, of course, be removed before attempting the experiment.

BALANCING AN EGG

COLUMBUS'S method of balancing an egg on end is rather well known nowadays, though it was doubtless the last word in Fifteenth Century pocket tricks. Columbus succeeded by shaking the egg so that the yoke was loosened and sank to the bottom, and this method can still be used, though the newer method here described is more mystifying, as the magician takes the very egg that the audience has been experimenting with and instantly stands it on end.

The secret lies in the use of a ring which is placed under the tablecloth. The egg is placed on top of the ring and is supported just enough to keep it from toppling over. It is a good scheme to have a thread attached to the ring so that it can be withdrawn unobserved at the conclusion of the trick.

THE FLYING PENCILS

THE performer passes two pencils, one red and one yellow, for examination. When they are returned, he wraps each one up in a piece of paper, leaving the pointed ends showing. He then scratches a small hole through each piece of paper, and the audience can clearly see the pencils inside. The red pencil is taken in one hand and the yellow in the other, and they are commanded to change places. Upon opening the papers, the change is found to have taken place.

The papers in which the pencils are wrapped are responsible for the success of the trick. Each is really two pieces of paper pasted together. In the center of each, between the outer papers, is pasted a piece of colored paper, one red and the other yellow, as near as possible to the colors of the pencils used.

The red pencil is wrapped in the paper containing the concealed piece of yellow paper; and the yellow pencil in the paper in which the red paper is concealed. Thus, when the audience think they are seeing the red pencil through the hole in the paper, they really see only the red paper, and vice versa.

THE PENETRATING PENCIL

THIS is a very clever bit of impromptu deception which can be performed at any time and in any place without preparation. The magician borrows a handkerchief and throws it over his left hand. He then asks for the loan of a pencil, and when he receives it, he pushes the handkerchief down into his fist with it so that it forms a little bag. Withdrawing the pencil, he inserts it once again into the bag formed by the handkerchief and pulls it right through the fabric, apparently making a disastrous hole in the handkerchief, but to the owner's relief he immediately shows the handkerchief to be uninjured, despite the fact that the pencil was pushed through it.

The magician, in doing the trick, takes care to throw the handkerchief over his left hand in such a way that very little of it is left hanging over the side toward himself. Thus, when the pencil is pushed down into the handkerchief the first time, the edge of the handkerchief on the side toward the performer will be pulled into the hand, and a small opening will be formed between it and the hand. When the pencil is pushed into the fist the second time, it is really pushed through this opening, though it appears to the audience as though it were being forced into the very center of the handkerchief.

THE CARD AND PENCIL BALANCE

THIS is a bit of juggling that will be found useful as a filler in between other tricks or as an impromptu stunt. The performer takes a pencil from his pocket and, holding it horizontally, succeeds in balancing a card upon it, the card resting on one corner only. Taking another pencil, the performer balances it upright on the uppermost corner of the card.

The card used is, in reality, two cards glued together with a piece of wire running diagonally from corner to corner placed between them. A small hole is bored in the first pencil near one end, and a similar hole is bored in an end of the second pencil. The wire in the card is inserted in the holes, thus making the balancing a by no means difficult feat.

THE LOOP AND PENCIL TRICK

A PENCIL to which a short loop of string is attached is handed for inspection and is found to be just as represented—perfectly ordinary and unprepared. Taking it back, the performer approaches one of the gentlemen in the audience and loops the string through his buttonhole. The loop is shorter than the pencil, and no matter how hard he tries, he is unable to remove the pencil without cutting the string, yet the performer does so in an instant.

The pencil is prepared by cutting a notch all around it about an inch from one end and tying a

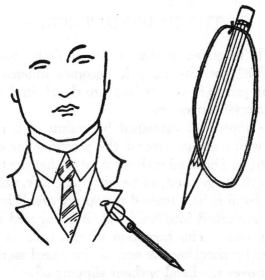

piece of string firmly around the notched part. This insures the string staying in place and not slipping up and down the pencil. The free ends of the string are tied together to form a loop about an inch or an inch and a half shorter than the pencil. To fasten the string through a buttonhole, place the loop over the hole and surrounding it and push the cloth up through the loop. If the pencil is then pushed through the buttonhole from underneath, it will be looped to the hole in a most inexplicable manner. It is a good scheme to cover the hands with a handkerchief while the pencil is being attached, so that the spectator will not see how it is done. Then let him try to take it off.

THE JUMPING PENCIL

THE magician pushes a pencil down into his closed fist. Suddenly it becomes imbued with life and jumps five or six feet into the air in the most unaccountable manner.

The impetus is furnished by means of a rubber band which is put around the second joint of the first finger. The hand is then closed so that the thumb covers the finger and, to be even more safe, the back of the hand is held toward the spectators. When the pencil is pushed into the hand, it is engaged in the rubber band. The execution of the trick is made simpler by notching the end of the pencil so that it will fit over the band without slipping off.

THE MULTIPLE THREAD

MOST people find it difficult enough to thread a needle a single time, yet the magician has no trouble in passing six or eight threads through the eye of an ordinary needle at the same time.

Take a piece of thread about two feet long and thread the needle in the ordinary way, leaving one end about four inches long. Unravel this short end by twisting it against the lay and pass the needle through it, taking care to have an equal number of fibres on each side of the needle, so that one side will be as strong as the other. You thus make a little loop, the long end of the thread passing right through the short end. Now pull the thread through the needle's eye, and each time the loop makes a complete revolution an additional thread will be drawn through the eye. This can be kept up until the eye is as full as possible, when there will ordinarily be from six to eight threads passing through it.

THE WATCH AND PRESIDENT TRICK

THE magician will need a few moments to himself to prepare for this trick, but if he sees that an impromptu performance is imminent, he can always take time by the forelock and get ready a few minutes ahead of time.

A watch is borrowed from a member of the audience and is securely wrapped up in a borrowed handkerchief. Each member of the audience is then given a slip of paper and requested to write the name of one of the Presidents on it. The papers are then collected and placed in a hat, from which one is withdrawn. The magician at once requests the audience to unwrap the watch and open the case when a picture of the President selected will be found within.

It must be admitted that the picture is in the form of a postage stamp, for this is generally the only kind that can be obtained at a moment's notice. Suppose it is a two-cent stamp bearing a portrait of George Washington. The performer writes George Washington on a number of slips of paper identical in size and shape with those he gives to the audience. The performer's slips are folded up, fastened together with a rubber band, and slipped into a handy pocket.

When these preparations have been made, a watch is borrowed, and while examining it "to make sure that it is a perfectly ordinary watch and unprepared in any way," the performer slips a two-cent stamp inside the case. The watch is then wrapped up and the audience write the names of various Presidents on their slips, among which there are certain to be several George Washingtons. While the audience are writing, the performer gets hold of his own slips and conceals them in the palm of his right hand. He then asks one of the spectators to collect the audience's slips and to bring them to him. He takes them in his left hand and pretends to transfer them to his right hand, in reality retaining them in his left and pushing the prepared slips to his right fingertips. This movement may be covered by turning away from the audience and walking back to the table upon which he has previously placed a hat. The prepared slips are placed in the hat, and when one of them is withdrawn it is sure to have George Washington written on it. The audience do the rest of the trick themselves, by unwrapping the watch and discovering the picture of our first President inside it.

THE DISAPPEARING THIMBLE

THOUGH in reality a piece of sleight of hand, this little trick is easily mastered and can be used to obtain some very surprising effects. The performer places a thimble on his right forefinger and apparently removes it with his left hand, but when the left hand is opened the thimble has vanished only to reappear from someone's pocket an instant later.

The sleight is performed as follows. The right forefinger on which the thimble is seated is extended toward the performer's left. The left hand then approaches it and closes over it, but under cover of the left fingers the right forefinger is quickly doubled in and the thimble is tucked into the crook of the thumb. The left hand is then withdrawn, being kept closed as though it contained the thimble.

It is surprising how easily the thimble can be concealed in this way and the right hand shown to be apparently empty. The thimble can be made to instantly reappear on the forefinger by a reversal of the motion used in making it disappear.

CATCHING A THIMBLE ON THE FINGER

FOR this trick two thimbles are needed, but these can almost always be obtained for an impromptu entertainment, no matter where it is held. One of the thimbles is secretly concealed in the crook of the right thumb. The other one is taken in the left hand and tossed into the air. The right hand is extended toward it, and the concealed thimble is gotten on to the right forefinger by the method just described. The second thimble is allowed to fall into the performer's sleeve, though it appears as if he had skilfully caught it on the end of his finger.

THE FLYING THIMBLE

THE performer shows both hands to be empty and then places a thimble on the tip of his right forefinger. Quick as a flash, it disappears, only to reappear at the same instant on the tip of the left forefinger. At the magician's pleasure, it flies back and forth from one hand to the other.

The trick is accomplished by means of a faked thimble made by cutting an ordinary thimble in half from top to bottom. One half is placed on the tip of the left forefinger on the back side of the finger. Thus, when the palm of the left hand is held toward the audience, there is nothing to be seen, but when the back of the hand is turned toward them, the thimble appears. The other half is placed on the front side of the tip of the right forefinger and is made to disappear by turning the back of the hand toward the audience.

THE THIMBLE THROUGH THE HANDKER-CHIEF

THIS is a new method of pushing a thimble through a handkerchief. In the old method, a second faked thimble had to be used, but in the modernized version of the trick, only one thimble is used, and it is unprepared in any way.

The thimble is placed on the performer's right forefinger and a handkerchief is thrown over it. The left hand, which has been shown empty, is waved over the handkerchief, and instantly the thimble is seen to have penetrated the handkerchief, still being on the forefinger but outside the handkerchief.

The trick is executed as follows. The thimble is placed on the right forefinger, but just as the handkerchief is thrown over it the performer extends his middle finger, and the handkerchief is really thrown over it, the forefinger being bent in toward the palm. The back of the hand is held toward the audience, and the handkerchief is arranged so that the greater part of it falls down over the back of the hand. When effecting the penetration, the left hand is passed in front of the handkerchief and the right forefinger is brought up outside the handkerchief. The left hand is closed, encircling both the middle finger and forefinger of the right hand, the thimble is lifted off the forefinger and placed on the middle finger. The forefinger is then bent down again, the left hand is removed, and the thimble is seen to be outside the handkerchief, though still mounted, to all appearances, on the forefinger.

THE COLOR–CHANGING THIMBLE

THIS is a very pretty color-change effect worked with a red and a blue thimble. The red thimble, which is on the forefinger of the magician's right hand, is taken in the left hand and at once shown to have changed to blue. The beauty of the trick lies in the fact that both hands are shown to contain nothing outside of the red thimble, first one and then the other being shown to be empty.

When the trick starts, the performer has the red thimble on his right forefinger and the blue thimble clutched in the crotch of the right thumb, or "thumb palmed." The left hand is shown to be empty and is then brought over toward the right hand. The left thumb and forefinger grasp the red thimble, and at the same moment the blue thimble is pushed onto the tip of the left second finger, which is bent in toward the palm to keep the blue thimble out of sight.

Now the right hand is shown to be empty and, as far as the audience can see, there is nothing to be suspicious about. The red thimble is then replaced on the right forefinger, and the blue thimble is simultaneously "thumb palmed" in the left hand. Everything is now ready for the change. The left hand is closed and placed over the right forefinger, from which it apparently removed the red thimble, but in reality the thimble is tucked into the crotch of the right thumb, and the left hand is withdrawn containing only the blue thimble, which is at once revealed to the audience, the red thimble being dropped into a pocket at the first convenient opportunity.

THE SEPARATED CORKS

THIS is a very neat after-dinner trick which everyone at the table may try his hand at, but it is a foregone conclusion that no one will succeed unless the performer tells how it is done, and even then many of them will fail to catch on.

Two corks, or, if they are not obtainable, two spools, are procured, and the performer holds one in each hand in the crotch between the thumb and the base of the forefinger. The trick consists in simultaneously taking the cork out of the right hand with the left thumb and forefinger, and out of the left hand with the right thumb and forefinger. When any uninitiated person attempts to do this, the corks always strike against each other, and it is seemingly impossible to get them to pass each other.

By following the directions carefully, you will see

how it is done. After the corks have been placed in the crotch of each thumb, turn the palm of your right hand and the back of your left hand toward you. Now place the left thumb upon the lower end of the cork in your right hand. Twist the left hand a little farther over toward your body, and place the right thumb against the outside end of the cork in your left hand, that is, on the end which is away from your body. Now place the right forefinger upon the inside end of the cork in your left hand, and at the same time place the left forefinger upon the upper end of the cork in your right hand, or the end opposite the one already occupied by your left thumb. If the hands are now drawn apart, the corks will disengage themselves and come free.

Once learned, this trick is simplicity itself, but it never fails to mystify the audience, who are all the more bewildered after they have tried to do it themselves and failed.

THE CANDLE AND FUNNEL TRICK

THE magician lights a candle and produces a magic funnel which he offers to one of the audience, at the same time suggesting that he try to blow through the funnel and extinguish the candle. No matter how hard the uninitiated spectator may blow, he cannot blow out the candle, yet when the performer takes the funnel and blows through it, the candle is immediately extinguished.

The secret of the trick lies in the position in which the funnel is held. The person who is blowing should be placed about two feet from the candle flame and will naturally hold the funnel so that the flame is in a direct line with the spout, believing that the air will travel directly toward the flame. This is not so, for the air will follow the inner side of the cone-shaped part of the funnel and will shoot off on every side of the candle flame without disturbing it in the slightest. To extinguish the candle, it is only necessary to point the funnel toward the base of the candlestick, holding it so that if the upper side of the cone were projected it would cut through the flame.

THE BOTTLE AND STRAW TRICK

THE magician produces a bottle and an ordinary drinking straw, or, if none is obtainable, a broom straw will do. He then challenges his audience to lift the bottle from the table, using only the straw to do so. The only feasible method seems to be to balance the bottle on the straw, and this line of attack is generally taken, but, of course, it is impossible, and the spectators never succeed.

The secret is made clear by the diagram. The straw is bent at the proper distance from the end, the distance depending upon the size of the bottle, and the bent end is caught beneath the rounded shoulder of the bottle.

THE BREAD AND NAPKIN TRICK

THIS is a trick that should be practised and learned by every prospective magician, for it is one of the most deceptive experiments in the entire realm of magic, and is suitable for presentation on any and every occasion. If shown at the dinner table, pellets of bread and napkins are used; if shown elsewhere, little paper balls and hats or pieces of paper can be used with equal facility.

The magician makes four small pellets of bread, each about a quarter of an inch in diameter, and places them on the table in the form of a square. He then picks up a napkin in each hand and places them over two of the pellets. Picking up one of the other pellets, he puts his hand under the table and exclaims "Pass." Upon lifting one of the napkins, two pellets are found under it, and his hand is brought up from under the table empty. The two pellets are covered with the napkin again and the remaining pellet is held under the table and commanded to pass through, which it does, for when the napkin is lifted there are three pellets under it. Now the three are covered and the remaining one, which has been under the other napkin all the time, is commanded to pass. The napkin is lifted and the pellet is not there. Upon lifting the other napkin, all four pellets are found underneath it.

The napkins are held with the thumb above and the fingers beneath and the trick is done by carrying the pellets to and fro gripped between the backs of the first and second fingers of the right hand. The magician first places the right-hand napkin over the pellet nearest to him on the left. He at once picks up this pellet between his right fingers, and then, apparently changing his mind, he moves the napkin over to the pellet on the right, at the same instant putting the left-hand napkin on the space that was occupied by the left-hand pellet. Thus there are two pellets under the right-hand napkin and none under the left.

The performer then picks up one of the other pellets in his right hand and puts it under the table. Picking up the right-hand napkin with his left hand, he reveals the two pellets. The pellet in his right hand is gripped between the backs of his first and second fingers, and when the hand is brought up it is shown to be empty. The napkin is then transferred to it from the left hand and is replaced over the two pellets. The pellet between the fingers is simultaneously dropped on the table beside them.

The remaining pellet is then passed through the table in the same manner, and when the napkin is replaced, it is dropped beside the three pellets already on the table. The other napkin is then lifted, and the pellet, which has supposedly been underneath it all the time, is found to have disappeared, only to be discovered with its companions a moment later.

THE WATCH, MATCH, AND STRING TRICK

THIS is a very surprising and even breath-taking experiment, particularly for the member of the audience from whom the watch used in the demonstration has been borrowed.

Borrow a watch from one of the spectators and tie it to one end of a piece of string a yard long. To the other end of the string tie a match. Next borrow a pencil and, holding it in your outstretched left hand, place the string over it, allowing the watch to hang down on the left side of the pencil and holding the match in your right hand. Move the right hand away from the pencil until the watch is drawn to within a few inches of it, and then ask the audience: "What do you think would happen if I let go of the match?" The only logical reply is that the watch would drop to the ground, yet when the right hand does release the match, it winds around the pencil and catches tightly against the string, checking the watch's downward fall.

There is no trick to this, as the results "work themselves." Just hold the right hand, which is grasping the match, a little lower than the left hand and place the string so that it touches the left forefinger, between which and the thumb the pencil is held.

The finger helps to deflect the match in the proper way. It is best to place a pillow on the floor beneath the watch until you have done the trick enough times to become proficient and certain of consistently successful results.

THE LINKING PAPER CLIPS

THIS is a pocket variation of the famous Chinese linking rings trick, in which a number of apparently solid rings are linked together in different patterns and formations. In the present trick the performer shows six or eight paper clips, giving them to the audience one at a time so that they can make sure that they are not joined together. When they are returned, he drops them into a glass, covers the glass with a handkerchief, and hands it to a spectator. When the handkerchief is removed, the rings are found to have been magically linked together.

The trick depends upon a clever, but easily executed, substitution. Eight clips, already linked together, are concealed in the performer's right hand, gripped in the crease of flesh at the bottom of the fingers. When the separate clips are returned, they are taken between the right thumb and forefinger and held so only a little of their length is showing. As the performer turns to pick up the glass, the separate links are moved back out of sight and the linked clips are dropped into the glass. Reaching in his pocket for a handkerchief, the performer drops the separate clips.

BLACK AND WHITE BEANS

THE magician requests the services of two members of the audience, to one of which he gives a small bowl and to the other a plate on which are a number of white beans. Without coming near either of his assistants, the magician asks the person holding the plate to pour the beans into the bowl and then to mix in with them a single black bean, which is lying on the table in readiness.

The magician then shows his hands to be absolutely empty and reaches into the bowl, immediately withdrawing the black bean. If desired, the magician's eyes can be blindfolded while he is performing this seemingly miraculous bit of selection.

The secret lies in the fact that, prior to the performance, a duplicate black bean was fastened to the bottom of the bowl with a dab of wax, and it is this bean that the magician withdraws. The bowl should be of a dark color, such as a jardinière used for flowers, and the performer should see to it, of course, that the person who is holding it does not have too long an opportunity to examine its interior.

THE END

A CATALOG OF SELECTED
DOVER BOOKS
IN ALL FIELDS OF INTEREST

A CATALOG OF SELECTED DOVER
BOOKS IN ALL FIELDS OF INTEREST

CONCERNING THE SPIRITUAL IN ART, Wassily Kandinsky. Pioneering work by father of abstract art. Thoughts on color theory, nature of art. Analysis of earlier masters. 12 illustrations. 80pp. of text. 5⅜ x 8½.　　　　　0-486-23411-8

CELTIC ART: The Methods of Construction, George Bain. Simple geometric techniques for making Celtic interlacements, spirals, Kells-type initials, animals, humans, etc. Over 500 illustrations. 160pp. 9 x 12. (Available in U.S. only.)　　　　0-486-22923-8

AN ATLAS OF ANATOMY FOR ARTISTS, Fritz Schider. Most thorough reference work on art anatomy in the world. Hundreds of illustrations, including selections from works by Vesalius, Leonardo, Goya, Ingres, Michelangelo, others. 593 illustrations. 192pp. 7⅛ x 10¼.　　　　　0-486-20241-0

CELTIC HAND STROKE-BY-STROKE (Irish Half-Uncial from "The Book of Kells"): An Arthur Baker Calligraphy Manual, Arthur Baker. Complete guide to creating each letter of the alphabet in distinctive Celtic manner. Covers hand position, strokes, pens, inks, paper, more. Illustrated. 48pp. 8¼ x 11.　　　0-486-24336-2

EASY ORIGAMI, John Montroll. Charming collection of 32 projects (hat, cup, pelican, piano, swan, many more) specially designed for the novice origami hobbyist. Clearly illustrated easy-to-follow instructions insure that even beginning papercrafters will achieve successful results. 48pp. 8¼ x 11.　　　0-486-27298-2

BLOOMINGDALE'S ILLUSTRATED 1886 CATALOG: Fashions, Dry Goods and Housewares, Bloomingdale Brothers. Famed merchants' extremely rare catalog depicting about 1,700 products: clothing, housewares, firearms, dry goods, jewelry, more. Invaluable for dating, identifying vintage items. Also, copyright-free graphics for artists, designers. Co-published with Henry Ford Museum & Greenfield Village. 160pp. 8¼ x 11.　　　　　0-486-25780-0

THE ART OF WORLDLY WISDOM, Baltasar Gracian. "Think with the few and speak with the many," "Friends are a second existence," and "Be able to forget" are among this 1637 volume's 300 pithy maxims. A perfect source of mental and spiritual refreshment, it can be opened at random and appreciated either in brief or at length. 128pp. 5⅜ x 8½.　　　　　0-486-44034-6

JOHNSON'S DICTIONARY: A Modern Selection, Samuel Johnson (E. L. McAdam and George Milne, eds.). This modern version reduces the original 1755 edition's 2,300 pages of definitions and literary examples to a more manageable length, retaining the verbal pleasure and historical curiosity of the original. 480pp. 5³⁄₁₆ x 8¼.　　　　　0-486-44089-3

ADVENTURES OF HUCKLEBERRY FINN, Mark Twain, Illustrated by E. W. Kemble. A work of eternal richness and complexity, a source of ongoing critical debate, and a literary landmark, Twain's 1885 masterpiece about a barefoot boy's journey of self-discovery has enthralled readers around the world. This handsome clothbound reproduction of the first edition features all 174 of the original black-and-white illustrations. 368pp. 5⅜ x 8½.　　　　　0-486-44322-1

STICKLEY CRAFTSMAN FURNITURE CATALOGS, Gustav Stickley and L. & J. G. Stickley. Beautiful, functional furniture in two authentic catalogs from 1910. 594 illustrations, including 277 photos, show settles, rockers, armchairs, reclining chairs, bookcases, desks, tables. 183pp. 6½ x 9¼. 0-486-23838-5

AMERICAN LOCOMOTIVES IN HISTORIC PHOTOGRAPHS: 1858 to 1949, Ron Ziel (ed.). A rare collection of 126 meticulously detailed official photographs, called "builder portraits," of American locomotives that majestically chronicle the rise of steam locomotive power in America. Introduction. Detailed captions. xi+ 129pp. 9 x 12. 0-486-27393-8

AMERICA'S LIGHTHOUSES: An Illustrated History, Francis Ross Holland, Jr. Delightfully written, profusely illustrated fact-filled survey of over 200 American light- houses since 1716. History, anecdotes, technological advances, more. 240pp. 8 x 10¾. 0-486-25576-X

TOWARDS A NEW ARCHITECTURE, Le Corbusier. Pioneering manifesto by founder of "International School." Technical and aesthetic theories, views of industry, eco- nomics, relation of form to function, "mass-production split" and much more. Profusely illustrated. 320pp. 6⅛ x 9¼. (Available in U.S. only.) 0-486-25023-7

HOW THE OTHER HALF LIVES, Jacob Riis. Famous journalistic record, expos- ing poverty and degradation of New York slums around 1900, by major social reformer. 100 striking and influential photographs. 233pp. 10 x 7⅞. 0-486-22012-5

FRUIT KEY AND TWIG KEY TO TREES AND SHRUBS, William M. Harlow. One of the handiest and most widely used identification aids. Fruit key covers 120 deciduous and evergreen species; twig key 160 deciduous species. Easily used. Over 300 photographs. 126pp. 5⅜ x 8½. 0-486-20511-8

COMMON BIRD SONGS, Dr. Donald J. Borror. Songs of 60 most common U.S. birds: robins, sparrows, cardinals, bluejays, finches, more–arranged in order of increasing complexity. Up to 9 variations of songs of each species.
Cassette and manual 0-486-99911-4

ORCHIDS AS HOUSE PLANTS, Rebecca Tyson Northen. Grow cattleyas and many other kinds of orchids–in a window, in a case, or under artificial light. 63 illus- trations. 148pp. 5⅜ x 8½. 0-486-23261-1

MONSTER MAZES, Dave Phillips. Masterful mazes at four levels of difficulty. Avoid deadly perils and evil creatures to find magical treasures. Solutions for all 32 exciting illustrated puzzles. 48pp. 8¼ x 11. 0-486-26005-4

MOZART'S DON GIOVANNI (DOVER OPERA LIBRETTO SERIES), Wolfgang Amadeus Mozart. Introduced and translated by Ellen H. Bleiler. Standard Italian libretto, with complete English translation. Convenient and thoroughly portable–an ideal companion for reading along with a recording or the performance itself. Introduction. List of characters. Plot summary. 121pp. 5¼ x 8½. 0-486-24944-1

FRANK LLOYD WRIGHT'S DANA HOUSE, Donald Hoffmann. Pictorial essay of residential masterpiece with over 160 interior and exterior photos, plans, eleva- tions, sketches and studies. 128pp. 9¹/₄ x 10¾. 0-486-29120-0

THE CLARINET AND CLARINET PLAYING, David Pino. Lively, comprehensive work features suggestions about technique, musicianship, and musical interpretation, as well as guidelines for teaching, making your own reeds, and preparing for public performance. Includes an intriguing look at clarinet history. "A godsend," *The Clarinet,* Journal of the International Clarinet Society. Appendixes. 7 illus. 320pp. 5⅜ x 8½. 0-486-40270-3

HOLLYWOOD GLAMOR PORTRAITS, John Kobal (ed.). 145 photos from 1926-49. Harlow, Gable, Bogart, Bacall; 94 stars in all. Full background on photographers, technical aspects. 160pp. 8⅜ x 11¼. 0-486-23352-9

THE RAVEN AND OTHER FAVORITE POEMS, Edgar Allan Poe. Over 40 of the author's most memorable poems: "The Bells," "Ulalume," "Israfel," "To Helen," "The Conqueror Worm," "Eldorado," "Annabel Lee," many more. Alphabetic lists of titles and first lines. 64pp. 5$\frac{3}{16}$ x 8¼. 0-486-26685-0

PERSONAL MEMOIRS OF U. S. GRANT, Ulysses Simpson Grant. Intelligent, deeply moving firsthand account of Civil War campaigns, considered by many the finest military memoirs ever written. Includes letters, historic photographs, maps and more. 528pp. 6⅛ x 9¼. 0-486-28587-1

ANCIENT EGYPTIAN MATERIALS AND INDUSTRIES, A. Lucas and J. Harris. Fascinating, comprehensive, thoroughly documented text describes this ancient civilization's vast resources and the processes that incorporated them in daily life, including the use of animal products, building materials, cosmetics, perfumes and incense, fibers, glazed ware, glass and its manufacture, materials used in the mummification process, and much more. 544pp. 6⅛ x 9¼. (Available in U.S. only.) 0-486-40446-3

RUSSIAN STORIES/RUSSKIE RASSKAZY: A Dual-Language Book, edited by Gleb Struve. Twelve tales by such masters as Chekhov, Tolstoy, Dostoevsky, Pushkin, others. Excellent word-for-word English translations on facing pages, plus teaching and study aids, Russian/English vocabulary, biographical/critical introductions, more. 416pp. 5⅜ x 8½. 0-486-26244-8

PHILADELPHIA THEN AND NOW: 60 Sites Photographed in the Past and Present, Kenneth Finkel and Susan Oyama. Rare photographs of City Hall, Logan Square, Independence Hall, Betsy Ross House, other landmarks juxtaposed with contemporary views. Captures changing face of historic city. Introduction. Captions. 128pp. 8¼ x 11. 0-486-25790-8

NORTH AMERICAN INDIAN LIFE: Customs and Traditions of 23 Tribes, Elsie Clews Parsons (ed.). 27 fictionalized essays by noted anthropologists examine religion, customs, government, additional facets of life among the Winnebago, Crow, Zuni, Eskimo, other tribes. 480pp. 6⅛ x 9¼. 0-486-27377-6

TECHNICAL MANUAL AND DICTIONARY OF CLASSICAL BALLET, Gail Grant. Defines, explains, comments on steps, movements, poses and concepts. 15-page pictorial section. Basic book for student, viewer. 127pp. 5⅜ x 8½. 0-486-21843-0

THE MALE AND FEMALE FIGURE IN MOTION: 60 Classic Photographic Sequences, Eadweard Muybridge. 60 true-action photographs of men and women walking, running, climbing, bending, turning, etc., reproduced from rare 19th-century masterpiece. vi + 121pp. 9 x 12. 0-486-24745-7

ANIMALS: 1,419 Copyright-Free Illustrations of Mammals, Birds, Fish, Insects, etc., Jim Harter (ed.). Clear wood engravings present, in extremely lifelike poses, over 1,000 species of animals. One of the most extensive pictorial sourcebooks of its kind. Captions. Index. 284pp. 9 x 12. 0-486-23766-4

1001 QUESTIONS ANSWERED ABOUT THE SEASHORE, N. J. Berrill and Jacquelyn Berrill. Queries answered about dolphins, sea snails, sponges, starfish, fishes, shore birds, many others. Covers appearance, breeding, growth, feeding, much more. 305pp. 5¼ x 8¼. 0-486-23366-9

ATTRACTING BIRDS TO YOUR YARD, William J. Weber. Easy-to-follow guide offers advice on how to attract the greatest diversity of birds: birdhouses, feeders, water and waterers, much more. 96pp. 5³⁄₁₆ x 8¼. 0-486-28927-3

MEDICINAL AND OTHER USES OF NORTH AMERICAN PLANTS: A Historical Survey with Special Reference to the Eastern Indian Tribes, Charlotte Erichsen-Brown. Chronological historical citations document 500 years of usage of plants, trees, shrubs native to eastern Canada, northeastern U.S. Also complete identifying information. 343 illustrations. 544pp. 6½ x 9¼. 0-486-25951-X

STORYBOOK MAZES, Dave Phillips. 23 stories and mazes on two-page spreads: Wizard of Oz, Treasure Island, Robin Hood, etc. Solutions. 64pp. 8¼ x 11. 0-486-23628-5

AMERICAN NEGRO SONGS: 230 Folk Songs and Spirituals, Religious and Secular, John W. Work. This authoritative study traces the African influences of songs sung and played by black Americans at work, in church, and as entertainment. The author discusses the lyric significance of such songs as "Swing Low, Sweet Chariot," "John Henry," and others and offers the words and music for 230 songs. Bibliography. Index of Song Titles. 272pp. 6½ x 9¼. 0-486-40271-1

MOVIE-STAR PORTRAITS OF THE FORTIES, John Kobal (ed.). 163 glamor, studio photos of 106 stars of the 1940s: Rita Hayworth, Ava Gardner, Marlon Brando, Clark Gable, many more. 176pp. 8⅜ x 11¼. 0-486-23546-7

YEKL and THE IMPORTED BRIDEGROOM AND OTHER STORIES OF YIDDISH NEW YORK, Abraham Cahan. Film Hester Street based on Yekl (1896). Novel, other stories among first about Jewish immigrants on N.Y.'s East Side. 240pp. 5⅜ x 8½. 0-486-22427-9

SELECTED POEMS, Walt Whitman. Generous sampling from Leaves of Grass. Twenty-four poems include "I Hear America Singing," "Song of the Open Road," "I Sing the Body Electric," "When Lilacs Last in the Dooryard Bloom'd," "O Captain! My Captain!"–all reprinted from an authoritative edition. Lists of titles and first lines. 128pp. 5³⁄₁₆ x 8¼. 0-486-26878-0

SONGS OF EXPERIENCE: Facsimile Reproduction with 26 Plates in Full Color, William Blake. 26 full-color plates from a rare 1826 edition. Includes "The Tyger," "London," "Holy Thursday," and other poems. Printed text of poems. 48pp. 5¼ x 7. 0-486-24636-1

THE BEST TALES OF HOFFMANN, E. T. A. Hoffmann. 10 of Hoffmann's most important stories: "Nutcracker and the King of Mice," "The Golden Flowerpot," etc. 458pp. 5⅜ x 8½. 0-486-21793-0

THE BOOK OF TEA, Kakuzo Okakura. Minor classic of the Orient: entertaining, charming explanation, interpretation of traditional Japanese culture in terms of tea ceremony. 94pp. 5⅜ x 8½. 0-486-20070-1

FRENCH STORIES/CONTES FRANÇAIS: A Dual-Language Book, Wallace Fowlie. Ten stories by French masters, Voltaire to Camus: "Micromegas" by Voltaire; "The Atheist's Mass" by Balzac; "Minuet" by de Maupassant; "The Guest" by Camus, six more. Excellent English translations on facing pages. Also French-English vocabulary list, exercises, more. 352pp. 5⅜ x 8½.   0-486-26443-2

CHICAGO AT THE TURN OF THE CENTURY IN PHOTOGRAPHS: 122 Historic Views from the Collections of the Chicago Historical Society, Larry A. Viskochil. Rare large-format prints offer detailed views of City Hall, State Street, the Loop, Hull House, Union Station, many other landmarks, circa 1904-1913. Introduction. Captions. Maps. 144pp. 9⅜ x 12¼.   0-486-24656-6

OLD BROOKLYN IN EARLY PHOTOGRAPHS, 1865-1929, William Lee Younger. Luna Park, Gravesend race track, construction of Grand Army Plaza, moving of Hotel Brighton, etc. 157 previously unpublished photographs. 165pp. 8⅞ x 11¾.
                    0-486-23587-4

THE MYTHS OF THE NORTH AMERICAN INDIANS, Lewis Spence. Rich anthology of the myths and legends of the Algonquins, Iroquois, Pawnees and Sioux, prefaced by an extensive historical and ethnological commentary. 36 illustrations. 480pp. 5⅜ x 8½.   0-486-25967-6

AN ENCYCLOPEDIA OF BATTLES: Accounts of Over 1,560 Battles from 1479 B.C. to the Present, David Eggenberger. Essential details of every major battle in recorded history from the first battle of Megiddo in 1479 B.C. to Grenada in 1984. List of Battle Maps. New Appendix covering the years 1967-1984. Index. 99 illustrations. 544pp. 6½ x 9¼.   0-486-24913-1

SAILING ALONE AROUND THE WORLD, Captain Joshua Slocum. First man to sail around the world, alone, in small boat. One of great feats of seamanship told in delightful manner. 67 illustrations. 294pp. 5⅜ x 8½.   0-486-20326-3

ANARCHISM AND OTHER ESSAYS, Emma Goldman. Powerful, penetrating, prophetic essays on direct action, role of minorities, prison reform, puritan hypocrisy, violence, etc. 271pp. 5⅜ x 8½.   0-486-22484-8

MYTHS OF THE HINDUS AND BUDDHISTS, Ananda K. Coomaraswamy and Sister Nivedita. Great stories of the epics; deeds of Krishna, Shiva, taken from puranas, Vedas, folk tales; etc. 32 illustrations. 400pp. 5⅜ x 8½.   0-486-21759-0

MY BONDAGE AND MY FREEDOM, Frederick Douglass. Born a slave, Douglass became outspoken force in antislavery movement. The best of Douglass' autobiographies. Graphic description of slave life. 464pp. 5⅜ x 8½.   0-486-22457-0

FOLLOWING THE EQUATOR: A Journey Around the World, Mark Twain. Fascinating humorous account of 1897 voyage to Hawaii, Australia, India, New Zealand, etc. Ironic, bemused reports on peoples, customs, climate, flora and fauna, politics, much more. 197 illustrations. 720pp. 5⅜ x 8½.   0-486-26113-1

THE PEOPLE CALLED SHAKERS, Edward D. Andrews. Definitive study of Shakers: origins, beliefs, practices, dances, social organization, furniture and crafts, etc. 33 illustrations. 351pp. 5⅜ x 8½.   0-486-21081-2

THE MYTHS OF GREECE AND ROME, H. A. Guerber. A classic of mythology, generously illustrated, long prized for its simple, graphic, accurate retelling of the principal myths of Greece and Rome, and for its commentary on their origins and significance. With 64 illustrations by Michelangelo, Raphael, Titian, Rubens, Canova, Bernini and others. 480pp. 5⅜ x 8½.   0-486-27584-1

PSYCHOLOGY OF MUSIC, Carl E. Seashore. Classic work discusses music as a medium from psychological viewpoint. Clear treatment of physical acoustics, auditory apparatus, sound perception, development of musical skills, nature of musical feeling, host of other topics. 88 figures. 408pp. 5⅜ x 8½.　　　　0-486-21851-1

LIFE IN ANCIENT EGYPT, Adolf Erman. Fullest, most thorough, detailed older account with much not in more recent books, domestic life, religion, magic, medicine, commerce, much more. Many illustrations reproduce tomb paintings, carvings, hieroglyphs, etc. 597pp. 5⅜ x 8½.　　　　0-486-22632-8

SUNDIALS, Their Theory and Construction, Albert Waugh. Far and away the best, most thorough coverage of ideas, mathematics concerned, types, construction, adjusting anywhere. Simple, nontechnical treatment allows even children to build several of these dials. Over 100 illustrations. 230pp. 5⅜ x 8½.　　　　0-486-22947-5

THEORETICAL HYDRODYNAMICS, L. M. Milne-Thomson. Classic exposition of the mathematical theory of fluid motion, applicable to both hydrodynamics and aerodynamics. Over 600 exercises. 768pp. 6⅛ x 9¼.　　　　0-486-68970-0

OLD-TIME VIGNETTES IN FULL COLOR, Carol Belanger Grafton (ed.). Over 390 charming, often sentimental illustrations, selected from archives of Victorian graphics—pretty women posing, children playing, food, flowers, kittens and puppies, smiling cherubs, birds and butterflies, much more. All copyright-free. 48pp. 9¼ x 12¼.　　　　0-486-27269-9

PERSPECTIVE FOR ARTISTS, Rex Vicat Cole. Depth, perspective of sky and sea, shadows, much more, not usually covered. 391 diagrams, 81 reproductions of drawings and paintings. 279pp. 5⅜ x 8½.　　　　0-486-22487-2

DRAWING THE LIVING FIGURE, Joseph Sheppard. Innovative approach to artistic anatomy focuses on specifics of surface anatomy, rather than muscles and bones. Over 170 drawings of live models in front, back and side views, and in widely varying poses. Accompanying diagrams. 177 illustrations. Introduction. Index. 144pp. 8⅜ x11¼.　　　　0-486-26723-7

GOTHIC AND OLD ENGLISH ALPHABETS: 100 Complete Fonts, Dan X. Solo. Add power, elegance to posters, signs, other graphics with 100 stunning copyright-free alphabets: Blackstone, Dolbey, Germania, 97 more—including many lower-case, numerals, punctuation marks. 104pp. 8⅛ x 11.　　　　0-486-24695-7

THE BOOK OF WOOD CARVING, Charles Marshall Sayers. Finest book for beginners discusses fundamentals and offers 34 designs. "Absolutely first rate . . . well thought out and well executed."–E. J. Tangerman. 118pp. 7¾ x 10⅝. 0-486-23654-4

ILLUSTRATED CATALOG OF CIVIL WAR MILITARY GOODS: Union Army Weapons, Insignia, Uniform Accessories, and Other Equipment, Schuyler, Hartley, and Graham. Rare, profusely illustrated 1846 catalog includes Union Army uniform and dress regulations, arms and ammunition, coats, insignia, flags, swords, rifles, etc. 226 illustrations. 160pp. 9 x 12.　　　　0-486-24939-5

WOMEN'S FASHIONS OF THE EARLY 1900s: An Unabridged Republication of "New York Fashions, 1909," National Cloak & Suit Co. Rare catalog of mail-order fashions documents women's and children's clothing styles shortly after the turn of the century. Captions offer full descriptions, prices. Invaluable resource for fashion, costume historians. Approximately 725 illustrations. 128pp. 8⅜ x 11¼.

0-486-27276-1

HOW TO DO BEADWORK, Mary White. Fundamental book on craft from simple projects to five-bead chains and woven works. 106 illustrations. 142pp. 5⅜ x 8. 0-486-20697-1

THE 1912 AND 1915 GUSTAV STICKLEY FURNITURE CATALOGS, Gustav Stickley. With over 200 detailed illustrations and descriptions, these two catalogs are essential reading and reference materials and identification guides for Stickley furniture. Captions cite materials, dimensions and prices. 112pp. 6½ x 9¼. 0-486-26676-1

EARLY AMERICAN LOCOMOTIVES, John H. White, Jr. Finest locomotive engravings from early 19th century: historical (1804–74), main-line (after 1870), special, foreign, etc. 147 plates. 142pp. 11⅜ x 8¼. 0-486-22772-3

LITTLE BOOK OF EARLY AMERICAN CRAFTS AND TRADES, Peter Stockham (ed.). 1807 children's book explains crafts and trades: baker, hatter, cooper, potter, and many others. 23 copperplate illustrations. 140pp. 4⅝ x 6. 0-486-23336-7

VICTORIAN FASHIONS AND COSTUMES FROM HARPER'S BAZAR, 1867–1898, Stella Blum (ed.). Day costumes, evening wear, sports clothes, shoes, hats, other accessories in over 1,000 detailed engravings. 320pp. 9⅜ x 12¼. 0-486-22990-4

THE LONG ISLAND RAIL ROAD IN EARLY PHOTOGRAPHS, Ron Ziel. Over 220 rare photos, informative text document origin (1844) and development of rail service on Long Island. Vintage views of early trains, locomotives, stations, passengers, crews, much more. Captions. 8⅞ x 11¾. 0-486-26301-0

VOYAGE OF THE LIBERDADE, Joshua Slocum. Great 19th-century mariner's thrilling, first-hand account of the wreck of his ship off South America, the 35-foot boat he built from the wreckage, and its remarkable voyage home. 128pp. 5⅜ x 8½. 0-486-40022-0

TEN BOOKS ON ARCHITECTURE, Vitruvius. The most important book ever written on architecture. Early Roman aesthetics, technology, classical orders, site selection, all other aspects. Morgan translation. 331pp. 5⅜ x 8½. 0-486-20645-9

THE HUMAN FIGURE IN MOTION, Eadweard Muybridge. More than 4,500 stopped-action photos, in action series, showing undraped men, women, children jumping, lying down, throwing, sitting, wrestling, carrying, etc. 390pp. 7⅞ x 10⅝. 0-486-20204-6 Clothbd.

TREES OF THE EASTERN AND CENTRAL UNITED STATES AND CANADA, William M. Harlow. Best one-volume guide to 140 trees. Full descriptions, woodlore, range, etc. Over 600 illustrations. Handy size. 288pp. 4½ x 6⅜. 0-486-20395-6

GROWING AND USING HERBS AND SPICES, Milo Miloradovich. Versatile handbook provides all the information needed for cultivation and use of all the herbs and spices available in North America. 4 illustrations. Index. Glossary. 236pp. 5⅜ x 8½. 0-486-25058-X

BIG BOOK OF MAZES AND LABYRINTHS, Walter Shepherd. 50 mazes and labyrinths in all–classical, solid, ripple, and more–in one great volume. Perfect inexpensive puzzler for clever youngsters. Full solutions. 112pp. 8⅛ x 11. 0-486-22951-3

PIANO TUNING, J. Cree Fischer. Clearest, best book for beginner, amateur. Simple repairs, raising dropped notes, tuning by easy method of flattened fifths. No previous skills needed. 4 illustrations. 201pp. 5⅜ x 8½. 0-486-23267-0

LIGHT AND SHADE: A Classic Approach to Three-Dimensional Drawing, Mrs. Mary P. Merrifield. Handy reference clearly demonstrates principles of light and shade by revealing effects of common daylight, sunshine, and candle or artificial light on geometrical solids. 13 plates. 64pp. 5⅜ x 8½. 0-486-44143-1

ASTROLOGY AND ASTRONOMY: A Pictorial Archive of Signs and Symbols, Ernst and Johanna Lehner. Treasure trove of stories, lore, and myth, accompanied by more than 300 rare illustrations of planets, the Milky Way, signs of the zodiac, comets, meteors, and other astronomical phenomena. 192pp. 8⅜ x 11. 0-486-43981-X

JEWELRY MAKING: Techniques for Metal, Tim McCreight. Easy-to-follow instructions and carefully executed illustrations describe tools and techniques, use of gems and enamels, wire inlay, casting, and other topics. 72 line illustrations and diagrams. 176pp. 8¼ x 10⅞. 0-486-44043-5

MAKING BIRDHOUSES: Easy and Advanced Projects, Gladstone Califf. Easy-to-follow instructions include diagrams for everything from a one-room house for bluebirds to a forty-two-room structure for purple martins. 56 plates; 4 figures. 80pp. 8¾ x 6⅜. 0-486-44183-0

LITTLE BOOK OF LOG CABINS: How to Build and Furnish Them, William S. Wicks. Handy how-to manual, with instructions and illustrations for building cabins in the Adirondack style, fireplaces, stairways, furniture, beamed ceilings, and more. 102 line drawings. 96pp. 8¾ x 6⅜. 0-486-44259-4

THE SEASONS OF AMERICA PAST, Eric Sloane. From "sugaring time" and strawberry picking to Indian summer and fall harvest, a whole year's activities described in charming prose and enhanced with 79 of the author's own illustrations. 160pp. 8¼ x 11. 0-486-44220-9

THE METROPOLIS OF TOMORROW, Hugh Ferriss. Generous, prophetic vision of the metropolis of the future, as perceived in 1929. Powerful illustrations of towering structures, wide avenues, and rooftop parks–all features in many of today's modern cities. 59 illustrations. 144pp. 8¼ x 11. 0-486-43727-2

THE PATH TO ROME, Hilaire Belloc. This 1902 memoir abounds in lively vignettes from a vanished time, recounting a pilgrimage on foot across the Alps and Apennines in order to "see all Europe which the Christian Faith has saved." 77 of the author's original line drawings complement his sparkling prose. 272pp. 5⅜ x 8½. 0-486-44001-X

THE HISTORY OF RASSELAS: Prince of Abissinia, Samuel Johnson. Distinguished English writer attacks eighteenth-century optimism and man's unrealistic estimates of what life has to offer. 112pp. 5⅜ x 8½. 0-486-44094-X

A VOYAGE TO ARCTURUS, David Lindsay. A brilliant flight of pure fancy, where wild creatures crowd the fantastic landscape and demented torturers dominate victims with their bizarre mental powers. 272pp. 5⅜ x 8½. 0-486-44198-9

Paperbound unless otherwise indicated. Available at your book dealer, online at **www.doverpublications.com**, or by writing to Dept. GI, Dover Publications, Inc., 31 East 2nd Street, Mineola, NY 11501. For current price information or for free catalogs (please indicate field of interest), write to Dover Publications or log on to **www.doverpublications.com** and see every Dover book in print. Dover publishes more than 500 books each year on science, elementary and advanced mathematics, biology, music, art, literary history, social sciences, and other areas.